Overthinking

Stop! Change Your Thoughts, Declutter Your Mind and Rewire Your Brain. Mindfulness Technique to Relieve Anxiety, Stop Worrying and Think Positively. Problem Solving Tips for a Happier life

By Albert Dales

© Copyright 2019 by Albert Dales - All rights reserved.

The content contained within this book may not be reproduced, duplicated or transmitted without direct written permission from the author or the publisher.

Under no circumstances will any blame or legal responsibility be held against the publisher, or author, for any damages, reparation, or monetary loss due to the information contained within this book. Either directly or indirectly.

Legal Notice:

This book is copyright protected. This book is only for personal use. You cannot amend, distribute, sell, use, quote or paraphrase any part, or the content within this book, without the consent of the author or publisher.

Disclaimer Notice:

Please note the information contained within this document is for educational and entertainment purposes only. All effort has been executed to present accurate, up to date, and reliable, complete information. No warranties of any kind are declared or implied. Readers acknowledge that the author is not engaging in the rendering of legal, financial, medical or professional advice. The content within this book has been derived from various sources. Please consult a licensed professional before attempting any techniques outlined in this book.

By reading this document, the reader agrees that under no circumstances is the author responsible for any losses, direct or indirect, which are incurred as a result of the use of the information contained within this document, including, but not limited to, — errors, omissions, or inaccuracies.

Table of Contents

Introduction

Congratulations on purchasing *Overthinking: Stop! Change Your Thoughts, Declutter Your Mind and Rewire Your Brain. Mindfulness Technique to Relieve Anxiety, Stop Worrying and Think Positively. Problem Solving Tips for a Happier life* and thank you for doing so.

The following chapters will discuss the best ways you can get around the problems associated with overthinking and procrastinating in order to manage your time and energies a bit more wisely.

Overthinking is one of those things in life which may be causing you unpleasantness every time it creeps into your mind. In fact, it might even be limiting your abilities to make the most of your time and effort. Needless to say, overthinking is one of those things which may be holding you back.

Most people spend a lot of their time overthinking and failing to realize that they can utilize their time in a more effective way. There are many reasons for overthinking, but what people do not realize is that it is as dangerous as any fatal disease.

That is why this book has been written with every intent to help you focus on the important things in life; the things which you truly treasure such as spending time with your loved ones and dedicating time to your favorite activities.

Great care has been taken to produce a book which has been useful and informative. Please take the time to focus on each of the chapters as they are filled with nuggets that will surely give you insights you can apply to your everyday life.

There are plenty of books on this subject on the market, thanks again for choosing this one! Every effort was made to ensure it is full of as much useful information as possible, please enjoy!

Chapter 1
What Is Overthinking?

Overthinking is one of the most common reactions that we tend to have as individuals. Often, we mull over things that have happened, or we believe are going to happen. Of course, it is a valuable skill to have, to reflect and think about the things that have occurred in our lives.

However, it is one thing to reflect with the purpose of learning and growing from the past, and it is another completely different thing to constantly go over and over painful situations that we can't do much about.

Then, there is the dreaded future. When you overthink the future, you are often invaded by thoughts of what could be, or what might not be. You might find yourself constantly concerned about events that, upon rational examination, are unlikely to happen. Yet, your mind is overly active, worried about grave consequences.

In the present, overthinking might take the form of waiting too long to make a decision. You might find yourself being hesitant about what to do, or what to say. Then, before you know it, your opportunity has passed, and you are left with nothing but regret about having missed an opportunity due to your inability to act.

For example, you have been offered the job of your dreams, but it requires you to move to a new city. Naturally, you are inclined to do your homework and conduct research on the new city and company. However, you become paralyzed by thoughts about not having enough information on the new job. You are overly concerned about making the wrong move. Then, you think about past situations in which you may a wrong choice. Soon, you are so hesitant to act that you simply cannot work yourself up to saying "yes" or "no". In the end, your inability to act has led the company to pass on you and give the job to someone else.

As a result, thinking things too much, dwelling on the past for too long, or concerning yourself with the future in excess

may lead you to miss the wonderful opportunities that life
has for you TODAY.

Chapter 2
What Are the Symptoms of Overthinking?

From time to time, we all become consumed by a problem or situation which we can't stop thinking about. When that happens, there is no choice but to try and manage our feelings as best we can.

Here are some clear signs that demonstrate you may be going through an overthinking episode:

1. A basic quality of overthinkers is that they see the world in high contrast. This means that everything that happens is a tragedy. They are always thinking about the worst-case scenario even when it isn't even close to being that bad.

2. They crave for affection, yet they don't always get it. Often, overthinking is just a ploy to get attention. While this isn't always the case, it might be worth asking yourself if it is just the comfort that you seek.

3. They pay attention to others' assessments as well. Considering the opinions of others is crucial in understanding your feelings and what you can do about those issues which worry you.

4. Overthinking is often characterized by a pessimistic attitude. While it's perfectly normal to worry about things now and then, pathological overthinkers tend to be glass-half-empty folks.

5. These individuals may turn into a burden to their closest friends and family. This is especially true if overthinkers are unable to function properly in their usual, day to day activities.

6. An overthinker attempts to locate importance in all things. Indeed, everything is urgent, everything is a life and death struggle, and everything is headed toward a tragic end.

7. You are overthinking if something is at the forefront of your thoughts and you persistently go over it. If you find yourself that you can't let something go, chances are you are simply overthinking things.

8. Experience the ill effects of sleep deprivation. It is common for overthinkers to lose sleep on a regular basis. While it's normal when you have something important to worry about, the chronic overthinker will experience sleep deprivation issues as a result of their pathological worrying.

9. Overthinkers recollect each and every word and detail from a discussion. If you find yourself keeping a play by play account of your conversations, then there is a very good chance you fall under the category of overthinkers.

10. Overthinkers have trouble relating to others. These folks will find it hard to build lasting relationships especially if they are bent in seeing the worst of every situation.

So, if you happen to find yourself overly concerned about things, worrying excessively, or simply losing sleep on a consistent basis, perhaps it's time to look inward and find out what is really at the root of your overthinking tendencies.

Chapter 3
Signs You Are an Overthinker

1. **Chronic fatigue**. The brain is at its maximum capacity when overthinking takes hold of your attention. Since the brain is a power-hungry organ system, it consumes a great deal of your usual energy. Hence, you may find yourself constantly tired bordering on exhaustion. This is why you often need more sleep than most folks.

2. **Overanalyzing everything**. The chronic overthinkers make something out of everything. Even when someone makes a very innocent comment, the overthinker will find something and blow it out of proportion. Often, it is just a ploy to get the attention they crave.

3. **Dread of disappointment**. The knit-picking tendencies of the overthinker lead them to constant

disappointment. Since it is virtually impossible for them to take anything at face value, they will try to find the catch in everything. This leads to constant disappointment.

4. **Failure to be in the now**. The overthinker is generally concerned about the past and focused on the future. This leads them to forget about living in the present, that is, enjoying life's most precious moments, and the people around them.

5. **Continually re-thinking themselves**. In other words, the overthinker is constantly second-guessing themselves, making unreasonable criticisms about themselves and the things they have done or failed to.

6. **Constant headaches**. Given the fact that the brain is at full blast, the overthinker is generally prone to headaches. It is only when these folks are able to calm down that they find peace and solace in the world around them.

7. **Chronic sleeping disorders**. Since overthinkers are prone to insomnia, they tend to be sleep deprived until their bodies shut down. At that point, they may

oversleep as the body attempts to recoup precious rest.

8. **Stiff muscles and joints**. A chronic overthinker is in a constant state of stress. This may lead to maintain a consistent state of stiffness in joints and muscles. Hence, aches and pains throughout the body are very common.

9. **Living in dread**. There is the overwhelming sensation of impending doom no matter how cut and dry things may be. After all, there is always the possibility that something could go wrong regardless of how far-fetched it may be.

If you can relate to these characteristics, then it would be a great idea to find a person in whom you can trust, who can listen to you, so that you can ventilate at least some of your feelings as often as you can.

Chapter 4
Types of Overthinking

Overthinking is a point of view that is excessively mind boggling bringing about sat around idly, chance because of inaction and low-quality choices.

Thinking about an excessive number of variables in a choice without separating and gauging significance.

Blaming the basic leadership process so as to abstain from something you would prefer not to do.

Disregarding something you definitely know.

Sitting around idly and assets pondering a choice that shouldn't be made at this point.

Seeing issues where they don't exist.

Slowing down on a choice because of missing data.

You wind up making each circumstance in your life about 100x more difficult than it must be.

You can't release anything since you're persuaded that if you simply keep running over the subtleties a couple of more occasions, you'll at long last reveal some new comprehension of the circumstance or it will some way or another change the result.

You've most likely never been secure with a thing in your life. You've drawn nearer everything from picking a school and an accomplice to your outfit toward the beginning of the day and brand of bread at the market with equivalent degrees of tension.

You're always saying thanks to the companions who stick around to hear you think about similar subtleties of a circumstance or relationship over and over, and however you never truly land at a different end, only the demonstration of overthinking is sufficient for you.

Rest is the most difficult part of your life since laying quietly in obscurity is the main time you aren't diverted enough to not have the option to sink into dashing considerations.

If somebody ever parts ways with you/decays to go out with you, you persuade yourself this is a direct result of a hundred irrelevant stumbles you made.

You wind up tormenting yourself over each other worn-out side remark somebody makes in light of the fact that clearly there is some significance to be revealed, it's unmistakably simply an issue of considering it until you discover it.

Chapter 5
Causes of Overthinking

Overthinking is a purely psychological response to stress. That is basically it. When a person is stressed out in a situation, they tend to think about, ponder, and analyze it.

Now, a healthy approach would be to find a solution for it, deal with it and move on. However, the human psyche isn't quite as cut and dry. That means that depending on a person's innate traits, they will dwell on issues longer than others.

As such, a person who is far more analytical will find the need to deconstruct events in their mind so that they are able to understand what happened and why it happened. In this regard, the need to find the root cause of the issues which occur in life lead the individual to become engrossed with certain event. Over time, this constant attention to certain events leads to a full-blown obsession.

Here are three of the most common underlying causes of overthinking:

1. Generally speaking, overthinking stems from feelings of insecurity. For instance, if an individual has abandonment issues, they may tend to feel as though everyone is bound to leave them at some point. By the same token, someone who has been profoundly hurt in the past may become so wary of others that they feel the need to distance themselves from others in order to keep themselves safe. As a result, they are always looking over their shoulder, trying to figure out who is lurking by.

2. Other times, a chronic overthinker is simply seeking attention from those closest to them. This is due to the fact that they feel neglected or disregarded. Hence, the overthinker may begin to fabricate ways in which they can take advantage of a situation solely for their personal benefit.

3. Then, there is the very real possibility that a person is simply faced with a situation which they don't know

how to deal with. Thus, this leads them to ruminate over an issue which they can't let go due to their lack of understanding. When this happens, it is of the utmost importance to seek help before a small issue gets out of hand.

While there may be countless reasons why a person will become obsessed with events in their lives, it is important to have a support network that can provide emotional support whenever the individual is confronted with a situation that causes them a high degree of stress and anxiety.

Chapter 6
Relationship Between Overthinking, Anxiety, Stress and Negative Thinking

As we have discussed earlier, overthinking a specific issue that has got all of your attention is actually quite natural. For example, you are planning to move to a new home. In this case, it is perfectly natural to be overly concerned about such an important event. However, a healthy individual will let go of the issue once it has been completed.

The overthinker may choose to knit pick the event of moving to the point where they go over minutiae in order to seek problem areas to dwell. This is why overthinking has a clear correlation with stress, anxiety, and pessimism. In fact, overthinking tends to create a negative feedback loop; a negative issue leads to stress which leads to anxiety which leads to overthinking which leads to more stress which then leads to more anxiety which leads to more overthinking.

Do you see where this is going?

As such, we are going to pinpoint some of the specific attitudes which tend to fuel that negative feedback loop:

1. **Overgeneralizing**: This is taking one model and saying it's valid for everything. Search for words, for example, "never" and "consistently." Example: "I'll never feel typical. I stress over everything constantly." Reality: You may stress over numerous things. However, everything? Is it conceivable you are misrepresenting? In spite of the fact that you may stress over numerous things, you additionally may find that you feel solid and quiet about different things.

2. **Cataclysmic reasoning**: This is accepting that the most noticeably awful will occur. This sort of silly reasoning frequently incorporates "imagine a scenario where" questions. Model: "I've been having migraines of late. I'm so stressed. Consider the possibility that it's a cerebrum tumor?" Reality: If you have bunches of migraines, you should see a specialist. In any case, the chances are that it's something increasingly normal and far less genuine. You may need glasses.

You could have a sinus disease. Perhaps you're getting pressure cerebral pains from pressure.

3. **Concentrating on the negative**: This is once in a while called separating. You channel out the great and spotlight just on the terrible. Model: "I get so apprehensive talking out in the open. I simply realize that individuals are considering how awful I am at speaking." Reality: Probably nobody is more centered around your presentation than you. It might search for some proof that beneficial things occurred after one of your introductions. Did individuals hail a while later? Did anybody disclose to you that you worked admirably?

4. **Win big or bust reasoning**: This is additionally called dark or-white reasoning. Model: "If I don't find an ideal line of work survey, at that point I'll lose my employment." Reality: Most execution audits incorporate some helpful analysis—something you can chip away at to improve. If you get five positive remarks and one useful recommendation, that is a decent survey. It doesn't imply that you're at risk of losing your employment.

5. **What "should" be**: People now and again have set thoughts regarding how they "should" act. If you hear yourself saying that you or other individuals "should," "should," or "need to" accomplish something, at that point you may set yourself up to feel awful. Model: "I must be in charge constantly or I can't adapt to things." Reality: There's nothing amiss with needing to have some authority over the things that you can control. Yet, you may cause yourself nervousness by agonizing over things that you can't control.

Chapter 7
Dealing with Negativity

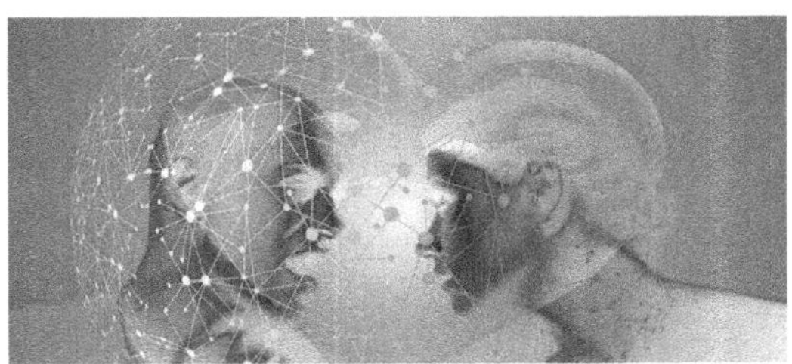

One of the most important things which any overthinker can do is accept that they are just that, overthinkers. When the overthinker sees the world for what it is, they begin a transition from focusing on the negatives of life to focusing on the brighter side of life.

The following is a list of actions that an overthinker can take in order to facilitate the transition from a pessimist outlook to a more positive one.

1. Be Peaceful and Smile

Smiling is one of the easiest and most effective ways to get you in a positive state of mind. Of course, you shouldn't do it unless it actually feels natural to do so. Nevertheless, smiling can help you trigger positive emotions inside you. This can then lead to a more optimistic outward projection. The end result may very well be that others catch your vibe making it far easier for you to get along with the circumstances around you.

2. Try not to Take it Personally

Learning not to take things personally is a great way to ensure emotional health. The fact of the matter is that the overthinker tends to take everything personally. What this means is that the overthinker will be concerned with trying to catch all the angles because everyone is out to get them. So, if your colleague doesn't respond, it's not because they hate you; it could be that they are simply upset over something else that happened to them. End of story.

3. Remain Patient to Create Space

Patience is a virtue. Overthinkers tend to be very short of it. This is especially true if there are situations beyond your control. Often, this tends to be the bane of the overthinker. For example, they have sent a job application and are sitting by the phone waiting for a reply.

Yet that reply may take a while…

Hence, impatience takes hold of the individual leading them to concoct all kinds of scenarios. These fabrications may very well drive the individual mad until the situation is finally resolved. That is why one of the most important qualities which an overthinker can work on is patience. As patience is fostered, the overthinker will be able to begin getting a firm grip on their thoughts and emotions.

Managing Your own Negativity

Learning to handle negative energy is an essential skill for all folks. So, here are some effective ways which can help you balance out your negative energies.

1. Use humor

While we don't mean taking things lightly, it is essential to try to find the humor in life whenever appropriate. Humor can often diffuse some of the tensest situations you can find yourself in.

2. Keep in mind, you are not your emotions

You are not governed by your emotions; you have full control over them. As such, don't be afraid to take the bull by the horns. You are totally in control of what you feel. Don't run away from your feelings; embrace them and try to learn from them.

3. Acknowledge that these emotions are temporary

Feelings come and go. Even if something is incredibly painful, the old adage, "time heals all wounds" is perfectly apropos. So, give yourself time to heal and let go of the negativity in your life.

Continue with Openness and Intention

Openness is more about giving yourself permission to feel what you feel. Don't run away from your feeling. That is only pushing the can down the road. When you feel ready, confront your feelings and learn from them. This will lead you to gain vital insights into your own self.

Chapter 8
Nature of Negative Thoughts

By changing your musings, you can change your emotions. While occasions are frequently outside of your control, you can figure out how to control your contemplations along these lines making increasingly positive passionate encounters.

We should take a gander at the attributes of negative programmed considerations to all the more likely comprehend their temperament.

1. Catastrophic commonly and foresees or expect a terrible result.

You consequently accept the direst outcome imaginable which makes upsetting feelings. Those disastrous considerations are frequently a significant wellspring of nervousness.

2. Its own.

You customize and appoint fault to yourself for things that aren't generally your deficiency. Adverse programmed thinking drives you to customize and acknowledge fault for things that are not so much heavily influenced by you.

3. Involve explanations like "should", "must" or "should."

Explanations that are confined with these words, especially when coordinated toward yourself, can prompt sentiments of self-fault, dissatisfaction, blame, outrage, and disappointment. These words ordinarily are unbending and don't permit space for modification for circumstances that change.

4. It's inescapable and tenacious.

One negative idea normally prompts another negative idea except if it's interfered. You can either nourish it so it keeps on flourishing or starve it by not proceeding to give the cycle what it needs to endure.

5. They generally make you feel awful about yourself.

These contemplations never leave you like yourself. You stress over not being sufficient now and never feeling adequate ever again. This makes sentiments of misery and vulnerability.

6. They are found out.

You structure ongoing examples of programmed musings that are difficult to perceive and in this way change. You can't change something you're not mindful of.

7. They will in general act naturally subverting.

At the point when a negative idea sneaks in, you start to feel frightful or stressed which affects your behavior. One of two things can occur. You don't make the move you have to take to accomplish a decent result in light of the fact that your dread has immobilized you. Or on the other hand, your activities are contrarily affected by the musings you have so the outcomes are undermined which further fortifies your negative programmed considerations. The idea of the cycle is horrendous.

8. Believable regardless of how outlandish they show up.

Programmed considerations have a convincing quality to them and you will in general structure your enthusiastic experience dependent on these contemplations.

9. They are one-sided.

You will in general markdown the positives and just feature the negatives. Because something you wanted didn't work out, doesn't imply that nothing will ever work out.

Hearing your programmed considerations is the initial phase in dealing with your most extraordinary feelings. Attempt to identify the idea you had preceding the beginning of your feelings. What were you thinking just previously and during the terrible inclination? Tune in to your inward discourse and hear what you're letting yourself know. You may think that it is supportive to begin an idea diary to record your musings. This will assist you with bettering comprehend the job your considerations play in your passionate encounters. After some time, you'll start to doubt your programmed musings and begin to address how substantial and genuine these considerations are. To diminish the recurrence of excruciating feelings, you have to tune in to what you think and ask yourself how legitimate these musings are. Keep in mind, what you think about last makes what you feel.

Chapter 9
Anxiety
Change Negative Thoughts

Anxiety is generally brought on by negative thoughts and vice-versa. When you dwell on the negatives, anxiety tends to shoot through the roof. Hence, the following strategies will help you get a handle on your negative thoughts thereby curbing your anxiety.

Thought Journals

Thought diaries chip away at a similar reason. They offer you the chance to get outside of your musings and get a progressively target viewpoint on them. First, you identify the substance of your negative musings, and after that, you record them in your diary. This makes you mindful of your considerations, gets you outside of them and enables you to survey them and choose whether or not they are valid.

Contemplation

Contemplation implies analyzing past, and current, events in order to distill valuable lessons from them. If you simply dwell on how miserable a situation made you feel, then you will only be fueling negative feelings inside of you. So, the next time something negative happens, don't be afraid to sit down and deconstruct why it happened. Then, take the most valuable lessons and put them to good use.

Intellectual Behavioral Therapy and Cognitive Restructuring

Psychological rebuilding is a procedure where you identify your negative idea examples and afterward question them. As such, subjective rebuilding is a procedure where you research your negative musings and build up that they are not valid.

There are five phases to intellectual rebuilding:

1. **Question** - This is exactly what it seems like. Evaluate your negative considerations if you think they are not valid. Challenge them. If you will, in general, think you are a disappointment, review to mind times when you were not a disappointment.

If you will, in general, imagine that you are constantly a disappointment in social circumstances, review to mind events in which you and someone else felt near each other. By and by, this is tied in with figuring out how to quit accepting your negative musings.

2. **Identify and Record** - The main activity is to identify your negative musings and record them in a diary. Also, record the circumstance where you had every episode of negative contemplations and how the musings made you feel. This will begin the way toward isolating yourself from your negative considerations.

3. **Practical Goals** - Negative considerations are frequently the handmaiden of having ridiculous pictures of and objectives for yourself. It is possible that you should be extraordinary in all that you do. Or then again you may request that yourself be somebody you aren't. This sort of mental self-view is an arrangement for negative contemplations. You will regularly be a disappointment in your own eyes, and this will offer ascent to negative musings. Create sensible objectives for your work life and your public

activity. This will diminish your negative mental self-portraits and negative musings.

4. **Positive Thoughts** - When negative considerations come up, supplant them with positive contemplations. "I enjoyed myself at that last gathering I went to". "Last week's gathering, everyone thought my marketable strategy was brilliant, and we utilized the arrangement with a couple of slight modifications."

5. **Examine** - Analyze the considerations in your idea diary. Search for examples in the subjects of your musings. Do your contemplations make negative pictures of yourself? What are the negative pictures they make? Try to perceive what sorts of circumstances trigger your negative considerations. The vast majority of all, investigate the musings to check whether they are truly valid.

Chapter 10
Embrace Positive Thinking

What makes somebody think emphatically? Maybe a couple of us are that upbeat vagabond, whistling and kicking through harvest time leaves cool as a cucumber in light of the fact that our lives are regularly punctuated with extraordinary trouble and despondency. Be that as it may, how would we get back up again in the wake of having the breeze thumped out of us? Positive reasoning is something that really takes work. The best individuals are the ones that can likewise recognize the truth about life; a beautiful brilliant gift, not without affliction.

The indiscriminately hopeful individual doesn't see this and when they experience an issue, which they unavoidably will, it floors them. They didn't see it coming, how right? For they are indiscriminately idealistic!

You need a touch of cynicism to enable you to explore the world. Else, we wouldn't see the threat that is surrounding us, and we wouldn't have the option to investigate a scene in any incredible profundity if we constantly held a kind of Disney perspective on the world. What's more, we as a whole realize that is not how the world is. Yet, when things are going admirably, we should figure out how to outfit that and appreciate those minutes, since like the terrible minutes the great ones are brief as well. So, building up the capacity to see them when they are available is significant for your prosperity and emotional well-being.

You absolutely would prefer not to be the interminable doubter, that individual can never observe any great in anything and they are continually trusting that something wrecking will occur so it can reaffirm their perspective that life is 'a story told by a bonehead, brimming with sound and wrath, signifying nothing'.

Also, they are not extremely charming to be near, indeed, an innately contrary individual is debilitating to be with. Furthermore, it must debilitate to be in their headspace. Never open to the likelihood that decency and bliss are surrounding us. Be that as it may, you must be available to see it; your eyes can't perceive what the psyche doesn't accept.

Opening yourself up to positive considerations really expands the odds of positive alluring results happening in your life and consequently change how you see the world.

Can any anyone explain why a constructive individual pulls in other folks? For what reason would we like to be in their organization? What is it they have that is irresistible? What's more, how can it be that about every single fruitful individual has a positive perspective on the world and have a principal faith in themselves? What's more, by what means can we as a whole build up an uplifting mentality?

Think about the accompanying tips:

1. How would you like to think? What is impeding those musings discovering unmistakable quality in your life? It is regularly as basic as saying; 'I will be certain today. I will be available to the plausibility of something extraordinary occurring for me.' Negative musings can nearly end up like a companion to us, we can be hesitant to release them since they are so recognizable. Regularly we get trapped in a negative example of musings. It tends to be difficult to see an exit from deduction skeptically.

In any case, when we take a gander at how we think and why we figure a specific way we can begin to improve our point of view with the goal that it permits us the capacity to see the miracle of our lives and how to grasp the great occasions.

2. Think about how you think. Tune in to your considerations, ask yourself a significant inquiry, is the manner in which I'm thinking valuable or liable to realize a positive result or not.

3. Remember contemplations originate from you; you are responsible for them. It can regularly feel like we are a detainee to the huge number of arbitrary contemplations coursing through our brains. Be that as it may, we choose which ones are significant and important for us. Become better at altering your contemplations; focus on the ones that will improve your life, not those ones that keep you down.

Chapter 11
Benefits of Positive Thinking

Why have an uplifting standpoint in life, since you can? Since there's a great deal in it for you. That is the reason. Keep in mind, positive reasoning is believing that is naturally advantageous. This is the thing that makes it 'positive' in any case.

You've just observed the 10,000-foot view perspective on the three essential advantages: positive reasoning causes you accomplish something you need, encourages you feel better (or if nothing else better), and it's helpful and quickly improves your life somehow or another.

Be that as it may, you can burrow down further to identify progressively specific advantages that are likewise worth increasing in value. In view of this, here are a few advantages of reasoning all the more emphatically:

More achievement: having more vitality, progressively confidence, and increasingly self-assurance prompts more achievement

Better rest and wellbeing: increasingly quiet, positive feelings imply less unpleasant, negative feelings that can negatively affect your body; the outcome is you appreciate the medical advantages of positive reasoning, including better nature of rest

A progressively beneficial life: the more you increase the value of your life with positive reasoning, the more advantageous life is for you

More noteworthy certainty: the more you trust you can accomplish things (a typical type of positive reasoning), the more self-assurance you have

More satisfaction and happiness: the more positive worth that you find in life, the more joyful you become, and the more you appreciate life

Feeling more grounded: as your certainty and confidence increments because of positive reasoning, you likewise feel more grounded and all the more dominant

More vitality: positive reasoning frequently persuades and stimulates you to accomplish things

More genuine feelings of serenity: the better you feel by and large with positive reasoning, the more significant serenity you have

Higher confidence: the more worth you find in yourself with positive reasoning, the higher your feeling of self-esteem

Increasingly agreeable cooperation with others: the more you appreciate life and worth yourself, the more you will in general appreciate social connections

More noteworthy clearness of brain: since you have a decision, it bodes well to think in legitimate, adequate positive ways that advantage you as opposed to in negative manners that hurt you; this is an advantage of positive reasoning great worth considering

Does thinking positive have any kind of effect?

Completely. You simply figured out how you can profit by positive intuition from numerous points of view, so sure reasoning truly works for improving your life.

The most significant inquiry, at the present time, is this: would you like to think positive contemplations and turned into an increasingly positive scholar?

This is on the grounds that the most significant factor for turning into an increasingly positive mastermind is to just need to think all the more emphatically, and to be definitive about making a move to think progressively positive considerations, paying little mind to whether any other individual needs you to think all the more decidedly or not.

With this lucidity of the brain, you are as of now well on your approach to growing increasingly positive perspectives about things.

Along these lines, if you have just realized what positive reasoning is, your following stage is to study how to think all the more emphatically and how to remain positive regardless of the conditions.

Chapter 12

How to Increase Positive Thinking

1. Start littler than you might suspect – The "floss just 1 tooth" – approach

Make your propensity so little that you can't state no. If you do this, to begin with, you can concentrate more on structure a propensity, as opposed to on results or how huge your propensity is.

Another regular propensity that too few individuals really do is flossing day by day. So, my recommendation is simply to floss one tooth the principal night.

Obviously, that appears to be so ludicrous a great many people giggle. Be that as it may, I'm absolutely genuine: if you begin exceedingly little, you won't state no. You'll feel insane if you don't do it. Thus, you'll really do it! That is the point. As a matter of fact, doing the propensity is substantially more significant than the amount you do.

At this moment I'm simply observing one extraordinary minute I saw, toward the finish of every day. Once in a while it just takes a couple of words to share this, occasionally it's two sentences. I've fused it into my day by day routine with regards to sharing what I completed the Buffer group, so it's anything but difficult to recall and simple to do.

Beginning little has helped me to join the training into consistently so it's turning into a propensity, without stressing over what a major assignment it is.

2. Set up your condition

Leo Babauta consistently has extraordinary exhortation on structure propensities, and this is one of my top picks. Naturally, we attempt to assemble new propensities (or even break old ones), with huge effects on our current conditions. Condition for this situation incorporates the individuals we invest energy with and the messages we hear or let ourselves know, just as our physical condition.

The stunt here is to guarantee your condition is as helpful for you proceeding with your new propensity as could be expected under the circumstances.

3. Attempt to Meditate – 3 minutes is sufficient

Ruminating is valuable for the body and brain. It does not just improve care and positive reasoning while you're doing it, however, it has been appeared to diminish sickness and improve care and sentiments of direction in life as long as a quarter of a year subsequent to being rehearsed every day for a brief period.

Beginning little works for contemplating, too. Think about only 3 minutes, to begin with, which is anything but difficult to do and supportive in building up a solid propensity. Subsequent to setting up the propensity for half a month, you can gradually build the length of your contemplation sessions to a sum that gives you the most advantage.

4. Observe 1 positive minute consistently

Seeing the positive things that occur in your regular day to day existence has been demonstrated to be an effective strategy for expanding your positive reasoning. This doesn't simply happen when you're doing the activity: the impacts can, in reality, last any longer.

One movement that is frequently said to improve energy is to record (or offer with somebody) three things you're thankful for toward the finish of every day.

Chapter 13
Declutter Your Mind

Thinking about how to declutter your brain? Having a bustling personality can make you feel pushed, restless and overpowered. Fortunately, we've assembled a rundown of approaches to declutter your brain.

1. Put pen to paper

At the point when you're attempting to keep mental tabs on everything that is going on, your contemplations are probably going to get confused. Keeping in touch with them down will assist you with prioritizing what's most significant, which will make you feel less focused. You can check significant dates and updates on a schedule or in a scratch pad, and scribble down your musings on anything that is stressing you in an individual journal. It doesn't make a difference whether you utilize an application or simply get a pen and paper. In a stretch, even the back of your hand will do (however it's not our first decision).

2. Keep at it

Work a portion of the tips recorded above into your regular day to day existence to enable you to offload mental mess. Ensure you get a touch of 'personal time' each day with the goal that you can slow down appropriately. Much the same as tidying up your room keeps it from transforming into an all-out dump, reflecting, composing, ruminating and conversing with others consistently will help anticipate the development of messiness in your brain.

3. Be careful

We've all heard that reflection is a decent method to clear your brain and unwind. What you might not have heard is that there are a huge number of approaches to be careful. This implies you can search for a way that suits you. Some regular things to attempt are yoga, exercise and profound relaxing. Some not really normal approaches to rehearse care

are washing up, snuggling up or chilling by the seashore. Do whatever works for you.

4. Identify the issue

It's difficult to fix something if you don't know what's up. Know about admonition signs that your psyche is getting to be stuffed. Some normal things to watch out for are issue resting, poor fixation and not able to unwind.

When you've perceived that your psyche needs a spring clean, the following stage is to discover what's adding to the messiness. Invest significant time to think about how you're feeling. This will assist you with identifying what's worrying you, and why. After some time, you'll improve at detecting the notice indications of a jumbled personality and have the option to halt things from the beginning pleasant and early.

5. Converse with somebody

Conversing with a confided in companion or relative, regardless of whether on the web or eye to eye, can be an extraordinary method to clear your psyche, discharge a few feelings and get whatever's irritating you out into the open. It additionally gets a new take on an issue that is got you puzzled and is worrying you. If you're truly battling, recollect that you don't need to handle your issues without anyone else. There are loads of different experts accessible to chat with about whatever's stressing you.

Chapter 14
What Is Mental Clutter?

Mental clutter is the stuff that occupies room in our mind, yet keeps on living without rent as we feed, dress, and

generally deal with life. The stuff sends us on aimlessly throughout life, and in the long run, leads us down a street that goes no place quick. If we let it, mental clutter will move in and take lasting habitation in our psyche. With a little work, we can figure out how to rinse our psyche and push ahead.

Generally speaking, the mind's optimal state is one in which it is able to focus on the task at hand. For instance, if you are reading a book, then you are able to read that book without your mind making it impossible for you to concentrate on the book.

This is the crucial point in which you can determine if your mind is actually cluttered: you cannot focus, much less concentrate, on anything. What this means is that when you attempt to do something, your mind is always taking you back to that which is occupying the most of your mental real estate. In fact, mental clutter can get to be so bad, that it can limit your ability to carry on with a normal life. While this may seem extreme, the fact of the matter is that it can certainly get to be that complicated.

Dealing with mental clutter is like dealing with a cluttered garaged. At some point, you are going to have to throw some stuff out and keep the stuff that is actually useful. In other words, there will come a time when there are things that you need to let go of. In other words, there are things which you are going to have to let go in order to free up precious real estate for the things that actually matter. As you become more adept at this, you will begin to recognize which things you need to hold on to, and which things you need to deep-six.

Chapter 15
Causes of Mental Clutter

In order to help you sort out the clutter, it is important to recognize which things are worth keeping and which are not. In short, anything that causes you anguish, pain, stress or plain unpleasantness needs to get the heave-ho. Those things which fill you with happiness, joy, and satisfaction need to be treasured for what they are.

As such, there are 3 kinds of mental clutter that are especially harming, and which you need to drop like a hot potato:

Negative self-talk

Our convictions about ourselves, others, and the world can significantly influence what we state about ourselves, others and our conditions. These conviction frameworks start from numerous encounters we gather over our lifetime. Twisted conviction frameworks can likewise develop because of horrible encounters or interminable dismissal.

Stress

Stress is fear's first cousin. Stress is constantly situated toward what's to come. Indeed, in some capacity, we accept that through our stressing we can really keep certain occasions from occurring and control our future. I am not proposing inactivity or inaction as the fix. We do be able to settle on decisions—yet we can just settle on those decisions with the best data and direction we have at the time. Stress pushes our deduction into absolutes and keeps us from seeing unmistakably. At the point when we start thinking in highly contrasting, there is next to no space for inventiveness or critical thinking.

Blame and ruminating over past slip-ups/decisions

The blame game is bad enough when you play it with others. It is even worse when you play it with yourself. If you constantly blame yourself over everything that happens, there will come a time when it will gnaw away at you so much, there won't be much left. So, take responsibility when it is warranted and learn to accept that there are things that are simply beyond your control.

By learning to identify these prime culprits of overthinking, you will be able to stop them in their tracks as they approach your life. By getting rid of them, you will be able to give yourself a fighting chance at decluttering your mind.

Chapter 16
Practical Tips on How to Declutter Your Mind

So, now that we have figured out what mental clutter is, the question begs:

How could we escape this cycle?

It begins with a cognizant decision to change. Behavior change begins with our reasoning. Dealing with your considerations is a continuous, everyday procedure.

Keep in mind you past and develop from it.

Help yourself to remember how you adapted or left a specific circumstance before. You can expect that on occasion you will slip once again into old examples. This is ordinary—those examples have been developing for a considerable length of time. Stress and blame specifically are difficult feelings. At the point when you get yourself in an old example, ask yourself, "How's my self-talk?" If you wind up drenched in tension, separate your stresses into 2 classifications: those you can control and those you can't.

Track your considerations.

Watch the words that leave your mouth (I'm certain that perusing with life partners will have a potential volunteer to help). How frequently do you end up saying words like, "can't," "generally," "must," or "never?" These are absolutes that keep us stuck.

Guide yourself to Stop!

Whenever stress rings a bell, or you verbalize it for all to hear, guide yourself to Stop! Supplant negative considerations with positive ones. One case of a positive idea is a token of what you do have rather than what you need. This isn't just about cash yet, in addition, your aptitudes, gifts, capacities, companions, family, and supporters.

In essence, making a concerted effort to clear your mind of clutter is a tremendous first step which you can take toward getting a handle on overthinking. As you begin to sort out through the fluff, you will be able to make better sense of your life and, most importantly, about the people around you. Bear in mind that if there are people feeding that clutter, then it might be time to move away from them.

Chapter 17
Declutter your Environment

Thus far, we have focused on clutter on a psychological and emotional level. However, we are yet to talk about decluttering at a practical level. What this means is that no matter how much you strive to clear up your mind, you will always be haunted by your surroundings. As a result, you need to also declutter your environment.

Decluttering your environment means getting rid of things that no longer serve you. For example, it might mean getting rid of old newspapers and knickknacks which no longer serve a purpose. It may also mean giving away old clothes that don't fit or getting rid of painful mementos.

It also means moving away from people who are affecting you both physically and emotionally. In some of the most extreme cases, some folks need to move to a new home, city or get a new job. Indeed, your environment plays a huge role in how you feel and fueling your overthinking patterns.

A good way to go about this is to become methodical in cleaning up your personal space on a regular basis. This personal space includes your space at work and at home. If you resolve to clean up every once in a while, you will find that you are also clearing up space in your mind. By seeing the clutter gone from your physical surroundings, you will be able to gain a sense of peace and openness.

By the same token, clearing up space from people who may be cluttering your life will also give you that sense of openness and liberation. As a matter of fact, having "too many" friends can be a source of stress and anxiety due to the perceived social commitments that you must comply with. Consequently, you may be adding an unnecessary source of stress in your life.

By whittling down your list of friends, you will find that sharing with those friends whom you truly value and cherish will actually help you to heal that which ails you.

Chapter 18
Space Clearing

Space clearing means clearing the space on a vitality level. It is old craftsmanship drilled day by day in numerous old societies and there are various ways and materials utilized for space clearing.

The purpose of the requirement for space clearing is straightforward: similarly, as on a physical level you see the residue and earth gathering in your home because of everyday exercises, the equivalent occurs on a vitality level. You may not see the "residue and earth" of human feelings, however, they do gather in any space, so it is ideal to get them out routinely.

By and large, it is prescribed to do an exhaustive space clearing session at any rate once per year in your home, or after serious occasions with negative vitality, for example, a separation, for instance. It is likewise imperative to space clear a house that you simply moved in, particularly if it is a dispossession house.

A light type of space clearing can be utilized each time you clean your home on a physical level, just as when your clutter clearing sessions.

Locate your top pick, most pleasant method for space clearing and use it frequently. For instance, I realize that numerous individuals are hesitant to smirch their place, yet they happily utilize basic oils for a similar reason. For those hesitant to utilize the real wise smear sticks, you will be glad to realize that you would now be able to purchase a smirch stick in fluid from, in a manner of speaking. Which means, there are air splashes imbued with the vitality of sage smirch sticks, and clearly utilizing an air shower is a breeze!

Another way I totally love is to utilize the "blessed wood" from a tree that develops in South America. It has the most beautiful, purifying and uplifting aroma, feeling the vitality of Palo Santo is an unadulterated joy. Alongside savvy and lavender, presently I generally use Palo Santo sticks, as well.

By and by, I want to utilize a mix of space clearing types day by day. I do get a kick out of the chance to smear, yet rather than a major smirch stick group, I think that it is progressively charming to utilize separate little stalks of sage. Sage feels profoundly purifying and establishing to me.

After the savvy, I utilize a stalk or two of lavender similarly, and the smell is simply superb, calming and tranquil.

Simultaneously I have a little tealight light consuming and generally have my fundamental oils diffuser going, as well. This may sound muddled as you read it, however, I guarantee you it is exceptionally simple, brisk and agreeable.

Examination in different ways and find what works for you. For the day by day or week after week use, you need a simple space clearing arrangement that inevitably turns out to be right around a propensity.

Chapter 19
Minimalism

Minimalism is as much a lifestyle choice as it is a mindset. Minimalism means to go through life with things, and people, which really matter most to you; the things which you really need to live. What this means is that you need to have your priorities perfectly clear in your mind.

Furthermore, minimalism should not be confused with frugality or downsizing. For instance, it doesn't mean giving up your car simply because it's wasteful to drive a car. The fact is that if you can't afford to own a car, then, by all means, get rid of it and find the right solution for your budget. But this also means that you don't need to break the bank and buy the most expensive car on the market... even if you can afford it. If you are perfectly capable of getting by with a regular car, then that's where you need to be. While it might be tempting to go drive around in an exotic sports car, the truth is that you can do without it.

Hence, minimalism is about setting your priorities straight and spending your time, money, and efforts and those things which are conducive to achieving your goals and aims. As such, simplifying your life also removes distractions and sources that lead to overthinking.

Think about it along these lines: the less stuff that you have to think about, the less sources of worry you will have. Plain and simple. Of course, there are things which are essential in all of our lives. You need to identify what they are. By the same token, you need to identify those things which are not.

Another great way of framing minimalism is this: minimalism is the result of decluttering your life. When you get rid of all the fluff, you are left with the essentials that you need to live the lifestyle that you want... without unnecessary clutter taking up precious real estate in your mind.

Chapter 20
Less is more

This is a tried and true adage. Indeed, "less is more", especially when you are talking about curbing the possibility of overthinking. When you declutter and adopt a minimalist lifestyle, you become more efficient.

In a traditional sense, efficiency is doing more with less. This is particularly true in manufacturing. In fact, manufacturing is built on trying to reduce the consumption of materials and eliminating any kind of waste or residue.

If we translate this into real life, you will find that you can, in fact, do so much more with less. You are able to accomplish so much when you declutter and minimalize your life.

Let's consider this example.

You dedicate a certain amount of your waking hours to the various activities which compete for your attention. However, if your attention is pulled into 25 million directions, you will find yourself lacking the ability to focus on a single issue. This will lead you to take far longer to get something done than it should actually take you.

In this case, less is more when you are able to get more done in less time.

How is that possible?

It is perfectly possible when you declutter your mental real estate and allow your mind to focus. This might mean locking yourself up in your office and forgetting about the world around you for a couple of hours. Yet, if you are able to do this, you will be able to get more done in two hours than you would have been able to do in two days.

So, don't be afraid to declutter and whittle down on all those unimportant things which are competing for your attention. Also, when you become more efficient, this opens up time and space for yourself, your family and your personal pursuits. However, this begins with your ability to declutter and make the most of your most productive times. It might mean going to bed a bit later or getting up a bit earlier, but you will be far better off for it.

Chapter 21
How to Stop Overthinking

Overthinking a choice isn't just inefficient and thwarts you from gaining any ground, it can likewise cause some genuine wellbeing results, including expanded nervousness and melancholy, low quality of rest, and undesirable adapting abilities, for example, voraciously consuming food.

What's the one thing on your plate that you've been putting off settling on a choice on? Regardless of whether it's a basic choice, for example, picking which conduit cleaning organization to procure or an increasingly intricate one, for example, whether to acknowledge a new position offer, sitting on a choice can make you have an inclination that you're incapacitated. You let yourself know, "no more, simply pick one and proceed onward." But the subsequent you settle on a decision, considerations of "am I making the best decision?" begin to flood in.

Attempt these procedures to maintain a strategic distance from the negative outcomes of overthinking:

Timetable your reasoning time

One of the issues overthinkers frequently face is pondering their issues throughout the day, or at troublesome occasions, for example, during a significant gathering. To stay away from this, planning a specific time where you give yourself the opportunity to consider the issue you have to settle on a choice about. If considerations about the issue creep into your cerebrum before your booked reasoning time, letting yourself know "No, I'm going to consider that after supper, not during this gathering" can assist you with pushing those musings away, realizing you'll return to it later.

Put a cutoff time on your considerations

To evade over-ruminating about a choice, give yourself a time period to consider it. By letting yourself know, "I'm going to settle on this choice by 10 p.m. today and whatever I choose will be fine" signifies you are giving yourself consent to consider it, yet not enabling it to take over different pieces of your day.

Solicit yourself what a sensible sum from time is to think about this issue. If it's a little issue, for example, what paint shading to paint your office, maybe a cutoff time of 15 minutes is adequate; while a bigger choice, for example, regardless of whether to acknowledge a new position offer in another city may warrant two or three days of an idea.

Take a break

You know the articulation "dozing on an issue," well, that is on the grounds that occasionally we're better at taking care of an issue when we're not considering it. Once in a while, we settle on better choices when we let those thoughts permeate in our cerebrum. Giving the latent pieces of your mind a chance to work through the issue can give the appropriate response a chance to come to you when you're not anticipating it.

At the point when you get yourself overthinking about an issue, attempt to change the divert in your mind by proceeding onward to another subject or changing your physical space by taking a walk or moving your workstation to a gathering space to chip away at something different.

Know the difference between critical thinking and stressing

While for the vast majority of us, overthinking originates from a dread of the results of making a move An or B, the individuals who are constant overthinkers regularly accept that they can take care of an issue by proceeding to pound away, considering it. In any case, stressing isn't equivalent to effectively taking care of an issue. While harping on an issue, thinking "this is awful, I can't deal with this" or repeating things that occurred in the past are a useless utilization of your time, pondering what steps you can take to improve the circumstance or effectively thinking about an answer for the issue are useful toward pushing ahead. Getting to be mindful of when your reasoning is unhelpful and when it's effectively critical thinking can assist you with ensuring your time spent reasoning isn't simply adding to your pressure.

Chapter 22
Stop Over-analyzing Things

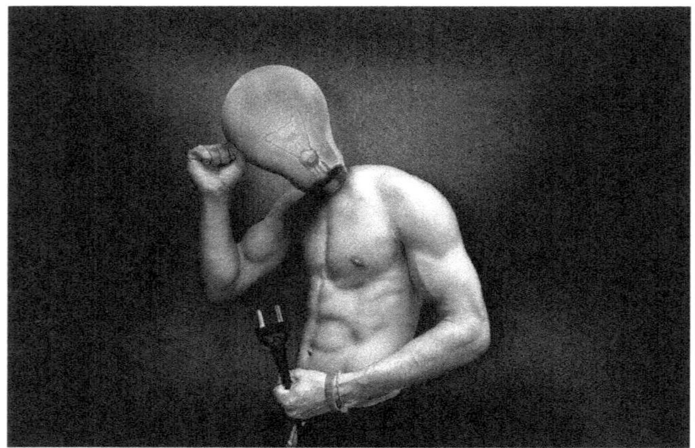

This is easier said than done.

It should be said that there is a fine line between due process and over-analyzing. So, how can you tell the difference? How can you tell the difference between doing your due diligence when something happens and when you are obsessing over it?

The answer is actually quite simple: when you find that thinking about an event begins to interfere with your usual activities, then you are overthinking. This particular event is taking over your attention. If this type of attitude renders you inoperative, you've gone too far.

Here is an example:

You had an argument with your boss. A discussion over a seemingly innocent issue got out of hand. You and your boss got upset and had a heated discussion about the situation.

Thus, you begin to fear the consequences of this situation. You begin to fabricate ideas of being fired or being seriously reprimanded. Perhaps your boss hasn't been too concerned about it, but you are now losing sleep over the prospects of what could happen.

Overthinking begins to take hold when you are unable to think clearly about anything else. If you don't take the necessary steps to remedy the situation, the thoughts occupying your attention will begin to fester inside of your psyche.

The solution might be as simple as walking into your boss's office and talking about the situation. Unless your boss is an unreasonable tyrant, they will be open to discussing the situation. It might mean having to apologize; perhaps your boss may feel compelled to apologize as well. At the end of the day, if you work things out, you can iron out any hard feelings.

As you can see, being proactive is one of the most important steps which you can take to nip overthinking in the bud. As you begin to think about things in terms of possibilities rather than problems, you will begin to discover the many ways in which you can curb overthinking and give yourself a fighting chance against overthinking.

Chapter 23
Stop Information Overload

Information overload can happen in a heartbeat. One minute, you're going about your usual business. Then, all of a sudden, things happen, you get a call, emails pour in and you are overloaded with information. Stress shoot through the roof and anxiety kicks into high gear as you need to deal with multiple issues at the same time.

If this sounds familiar, then you're not alone. In fact, it is quite common to see information overload at every turn. It can be daunting to think that you have no alternative but to deal with what's coming at you.

Well, there is an alternative. Always ask yourself, "what's the most important thing I could be doing right now?"

When you train yourself to always think along these lines, you will be able to make yourself productive and stay clearheaded despite the flurry of information and occurrences around you. By being clear on the most important thing for you at any given time, you will be able to sort through the flurry around you.

When you're not clear and what your top priorities are, it is easy to get tangled up with things that are not a top priority. The fact of the matter is that most of the time, many of the things which you are on your plate are not ultra-urgent. With that in mind, avoiding information overload is far easier than you think.

So, always keep your top priorities in mind. That way, when the action gets fast and furious, you need to stay focused on the most important task at hand. By resisting the temptation to multitask, you will be able to do more with less. As you become more and more efficient, you will see your productivity soar and your self-confidence spike. Please bear in mind that you don't need to do everything right away. Most of the time, you can negotiate deadlines and get help when you need it.

Chapter 24
Stop Being a Perfectionist

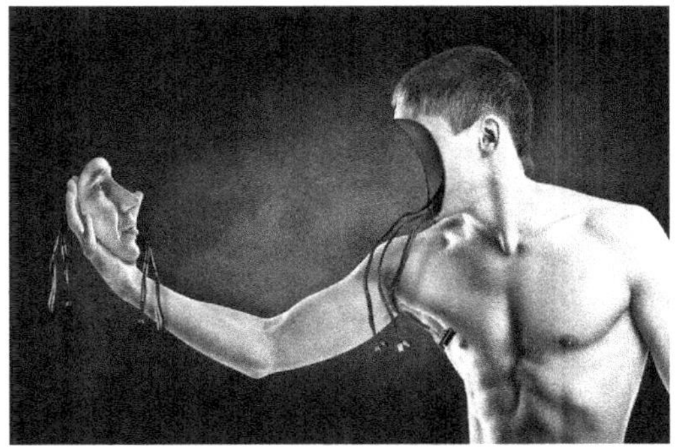

We all want to be the best. We all want to have the best. We all want to be the greatest. And while it's great to be ambitious and search for excellence, it can lead to putting undue pressure on yourself.

There is a very fine line between being a positive perfectionist and a negative one. When you are a positive perfectionist, you strive for excellence while admitting that mistakes are a part of the learning process that involved achieving greatness. On the other hand, being a negative perfectionist will lead you to become unreasonable and intolerant to mistakes.

So, what does that imply?
It implies that there needs to be a balance between tolerating mistakes and becoming a toxic individual. When you tolerate

mistakes within a reasonable level, especially from yourself, you are able to grow and learn. When you reach a toxic level, you put so much pressure on yourself, and others, to be perfect, that it just eats away at you.

A great example of this can be seen in parents who place unrealistic expectations on themselves and their children. These types of parents expect perfect grades, perfect behavior and perfect appearance from their children. Over time, this can become a toxic environment for a child. It may lead them to develop self-esteem issues while leaving the parent emotionally exhausted from all the pressure they put on themselves and their families.

The dark side of perfectionists leads them to criticize everything they do and second guess themselves at everything turn. Needless to say, that is hardly an environment which is conducive to personal growth and development. In short, we need to cut ourselves a little bit of slack, acknowledge when we haven't done out best and come back the next day determined to be better. When you are able to put past failures behind you and learn from them, you will be able to truly grow as a person.

So, take the pressure off yourself; you're already doing a great job.

Chapter 25
Stop Procrastination -- Analysis Paralysis -- Causes and Solutions

Procrastination, in short, means putting things off. What's wrong with that? Well, putting things off generally builds up pressure until one thing, or another blows up.

Think about this way: you see a crack in a wall in your home. Do you get it fixed or leave it that way? You could do nothing about it. However, it will eventually break and cause far greater damage than you had anticipated.

So, here are some great ways in which you can deal with procrastination and the paralysis that comes from over-analyzing things.

1. Try not to Believe Everything your Mind Tells You

It is perfectly true that your mind can play tricks on you. So, don't be afraid to listen to your gut every once in a while. You will find that listening to your gut feelings can validate a lot of your first impressions.

2. Change the Channel

Often, taking a timeout from the hustle and bustle of your daily routine is enough to help you regroup and gain the focus you need to solve the issues at hand. Don't be afraid to take a step back and breathe.

3. Know The Difference Between Thinking and Overthinking

When your thoughts are geared toward finding a solution, being proactive and dealing with situations, you are thinking. When your thoughts are about worry, concern, and fear, you are overthinking.

4. Try not to Make Mountains Out of Molehills

Everything that happens in life isn't the end of the world. While it is always a good idea to be prepared for the worst-

case scenario, the fact of the matter is that you will rarely
have to deal with the worst possible outcome. When you take
a look back at life, you will realize that things could have
always been worse.

5. Timetable Some 'Stress Time' Into Your Day

No, we don't mean you should make time for stress; what we
mean is that it is okay to get stressed out. When that
happens, take time to decompress and detox from the
stressful situations in your day.

6. Become Consciously Aware

Living in the present is one of the most valuable attitudes
you can take. Don't worry about the past because it's gone.
Don't worry about the future because it hasn't arrived yet.
Concern yourself with the present, the rest will fall into
place.

7. Settle on Time-Limited Decisions

Set a timer for your decisions. If something requires your
immediate attention, then do it. Then, you can determine
when something needs to be done based on its priority and

urgency. That will help you set effective timetables for your decisions.

8.   Set the Mind Back in Its Place

At the end of your day, do take the time to unwind and relax. Sometimes, it only takes about 15 minutes to regroup, relax and get prepped for the next day. Don't neglect downtime as it is important for the recovery of your energy and focus.

Chapter 26
Set Deadlines

Deadlines are not meant to constrict your life. They are meant to set boundaries by which you need to work with. Imagine if we didn't have deadlines in life; nothing would ever get done.

Think about that.

If you didn't have to pay your bills on a certain day, would you ever pay them at all?

As such, deadlines help us to organize ourselves in such a way that we are able to make the most of our time in a productive manner. By setting deadlines to important decisions and actions that need to be done, you will find that it will create the structure that you need in order to keep your goals moving forward.

By the same token, healthy scheduling means that you are able to set realistic timelines for your personal goals while managing work and school in a way that you can comfortably handle the load. If you find that you simply cannot cope with everything on your plate, then it might be time to rethink your approach and let go of things that are not conducive to your overall goals and aims.

Think about it this way:

You need to make a decision regarding your car. It is getting older and may need to be replaced soon. So, you set a deadline: "I will get rid of it the next time it breaks down" or "I will get a new car at the end of the year". As you can see, these deadlines don't necessarily involve time and date. What they do involve in a marker in which you have prompted yourself to act. So, when your car does break down, you know it's time to act. This gets rid of overthinking and hesitation. You know when you need to act.

Perhaps the biggest benefit of deadlines is that you can hold yourself accountable. So, if you don't meet your deadlines, then there must be a reason for it. You can then analyze why things didn't go down the way you intended them to as opposed to beating up yourself over it. That way, the next time you set a deadline, you know it is within reason.

Chapter 27
Create a To-Do list

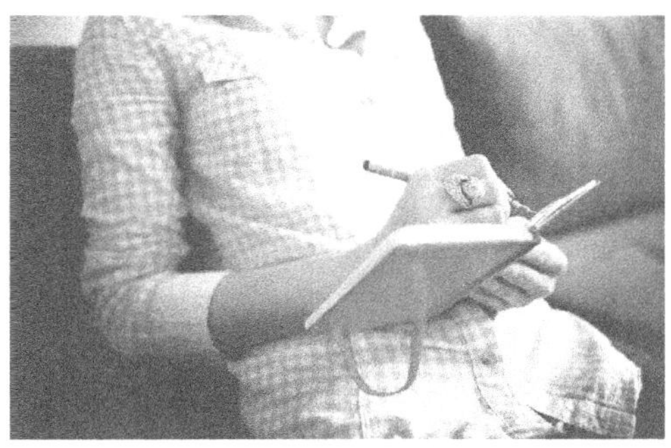

You might be thinking that To-Do lists are old-fashioned and old school. The fact of the matter is that they are relevant tools so long as you use them for what they are intended: to help you prioritize your activities.

Have you ever heard the expression, "that will go atop the To-Do list"?

The reason for that expression is due to the fact that the top of the list involves the actions which have the highest priority. If something gets shoved down to the bottom of the pile, then it means it is not as important as others.

When you go about creating a To-Do list, you are essentially ranking your activities from the highest to the lowest priority. This entails making an educated assumption as to what needs to be done, and when it needs to be done, and what can wait.

Another important value to the To-Do list is that it helps to create personal accountability. When you see that the To-Do list just keeps piling up with unfinished items, then you need to ask yourself if the items on that list really need to be there. If they do, then you need to analyze why they haven't been done.

Often, clearing a To-Do list might mean consciously making an effort to set time aside and drilling down. Many times, this is the solution to an unfinished list. If something doesn't make sense, or you know it doesn't belong on the list, then it might be a good idea to deep-six it.

Furthermore, keeping a written list such as in a notebook can help your brain fixate the things that need to be done on that list. As you actually write things down, you will be able to help your mind focus on what needs to be done. That takes the guesswork away, reduces stress and nips overthinking in the bud. You know what you need to do; so, it is only a matter of getting down to business.

Chapter 28
Evaluate Your Time Usage

This can be tricky especially if you are prone to distraction. When you get easily distracted, you can be sidetracked from activities which really matter. By the time you come to realize, precious time has ticked away on something which wasn't urgent or important.

In order for you to track your time usage, it is a good idea to make a conscious effort to take note of the time you spend on various activities. Here is a quick list of activities which you can rather easily track the time you spend on them:

- Commuting
- Watching TV
- Playing games
- Social media

- Socializing
- Sleeping
- Running errands

All of these activities, while important to a certain degree, can be tracked rather easily. In particular, commuting and sleeping are two activities that need a specific amount of time allotted to them. If you neglect sleep, you will pay the price over time. If you spend too much time commuting, then you might have to reevaluate your options.

The fact of the matter is that time allocation is a zero-sum game. This means that you have to take away from one activity to give to another. This is why prioritization is so important. When you realize what's truly important, such as sleep, you won't neglect giving it the time it deserves.

As you make a concerted effort to track the time you spend on your various activities, you may be startled to realize how much time you actually devote to activities that don't have much bearing on your goals. For example, you need to evaluate the impact that playing video games have on getting you a promotion at work. Nevertheless, if you play video games as a means of unwinding, then doing so in a productive manner will be helpful. Doing so in an unproductive manner will simply take attention away from what truly matters in the long run.

Chapter 29

Limit Your Media Consumption

Rehearsing care is a famous New Year's goals this year. Care as a hunting term scored a 98 a week ago on Google. The score speaks to the pursuit of intrigue comparative with the most noteworthy point on the graph, so care is certainly a present pattern. Similarly, contemplation scored 100 a week ago. Both pursuit terms scored close to 50 only five years prior.

I started reflecting a year ago and have thought that it was useful in various manners. It hasn't quite recently decreased pressure; I've additionally turned out to be increasingly engaged and beneficial at work. Contemplation is dubious, particularly for apprentices. More often than not, I utilize guided contemplation applications or digital broadcasts to enable me to center.

Quiet is an application I use, and every day it delivers a themed guided contemplation. So far this year, the majority of the topics have included basic New Year's goals, for example, substance misuse, indulging and negative musings.

The present topic was the careful utilization of media. Every contemplation closes with a statement, and the present was from self-improvement creator Mark Manson.

"Boundless access to learning brings boundless chance. Be that as it may, just to the individuals who figure out how to deal with the new money: their consideration," he composed.

Endless news sources and online networking channels, accessible every minute of every day on advanced cells, all go after our consideration. A considerable lot of these data sources are composed to mix an enthusiastic reaction to energize snaps or remarks since commitment is media cash.

A great many people realize that, yet they regardless enable themselves to get cleared away in the ebb and flow of feelings created by news waterways. If you read about deplorable events, rapes, and offending political spikes before you even get up, you'll likely convey those negative feelings with all of your days long, and they will drain the delight out of your day. Do this for a long time, and you'll before long find you're carrying on with a life bereft of bliss and satisfaction.

Restricting media utilization isn't simple. As somebody with a news-casting degree who has made her living in media and substance for a large portion of her life, it's very a battle for me. If you battle with careful media utilization as I do, here are three hints I've discovered supportive.

Join Facebook gatherings

In the course of recent months, I've joined Facebook bunches for exceptional needs guardians in my general vicinity, female entrepreneurs, online business suppliers, and otherworldly development. Posts from these gatherings currently overwhelm my news channel, diminishing the number of posts that don't create any positive or accommodating data, similar to companions or relatives contending about governmental issues. It's likewise decreased the time I spend on Facebook, in light of the fact that these gatherings are loaded up with individuals who are living rich, satisfied lives and they share ways I can do it, as well. Rather than getting sucked into careless recordings or negative political discussion, I'm propelled to put down my telephone and live right now.

Start the day accomplishing something imaginative

This tip originated from my Facebook profound development site. Research has demonstrated that if you start your day accomplishing something profitable and innovative, for example, working out, journaling or contemplating, you'll convey that outlook with you for the duration of the day. In like manner, if you start your day accomplishing something receptive, for example, understanding news or reacting to web-based social networking posts, you'll convey that mentality throughout the day. The previous is unquestionably more positive and satisfying than the last mentioned.

Breaking point your news time

One of the nifty devices I'm utilizing this year is a shape clock, which is actually what it seems like. It's a plastic 3D square with times on each side and a clock component inside. Turn the measure of time face up, and the clock will tally down and blare when time is up. I utilize the clock to enable me to concentrate on work errands, but at the same time, it's useful when devouring media. I just give myself 15-20 minutes of news time every day. At the point when time is up, I proceed onward. News locales like CU Insight can be extremely useful when restricting news time since you can rapidly filter an assortment of news sources.

Your consideration is important to cash. When you ace that idea, it will be simpler to all the more carefully expend media and select data that will enable you to live a more joyful and increasingly beneficial life.

Chapter 30
Plan Your Meals Wisely

One of the primary ideas of planning is figuring out how to oversee cash admirably. In any case, planning for nourishment can end up difficult as a result of haphazardly eating out or sporadic shopping for food. Truth be told, the spending plan for nourishment is likely the most difficult piece of making a reasonable family spending plan due to the consistently changing business sector and fluctuating costs.

Pursue these tips to make planning for nourishment somewhat simpler:

Plan Ahead – Planning ahead can help spare issues when planning for nourishment costs. Arranging every one of the dinners out constantly means posting your necessary fixings, computing the expense, and constraining eating out. Not exclusively does preparing help with the planning, however, it helps with the shopping for food also in light of the fact that the desires are spread out obviously every week. Supper arranging doesn't need to be difficult, and it can even be adaptable.

Make a List – For any individual who is beginning a nourishment spending plan, causing a rundown of staple goods to can be an ideal method to hold that financial limit under tight restraints. Start by experiencing the storeroom and cooler. Record the vital food supplies under one heading; at that point include everything else into a subsequent heading. By isolating needs and needs with regards to shopping for food, budgeters can wipe out extra superfluous spending. Close to everything, record an expected expense or real cost if known. If the expense is obscure, speculate. If one of the "needs" on the rundown doesn't cost as much as getting ready for, at that point, it is discretionary to buy from the "need" list.

Make it Flexible – Make sure the whole spending plan is somewhat adaptable. If spending isn't as much in another piece of the spending that month, take a day to overdo it a piece and have a pleasant supper out. If the day has been long, utilize a minimal expenditure to get some dessert or cake. If there is another eating routine in the arrangement, fix the nourishment spending plan to incorporate the costs of another nourishment thing. Whatever is done, make a point to be adaptable with the essential shopping for food and nourishment spending plan. It can spare a decent piece of worry later on.

Inexpensive food and café tips – Eating out isn't modest. Furthermore, if you do it as often as possible, the dollars truly add up. A worth supper at a well-known burger chain may just be 5 dollars, however, that is a great deal of cash spent on a moderately healthfully void passage. If you make every one of the three of your day by day squares inexpensive food, you'll be doing harm not exclusively to your cardiovascular wellbeing and your waistline yet to your wallet also.

Chapter 31
Simplify your Life and Live in the Present

Living in the present in one of the hardest things to do in life. It is not quite so easy to go through not thinking about the past or the future. In fact, we spend most of our lives remembering the past and planning for the future. In the meantime, we tend to forget about what's actually going on at the present time.

When you practice living in the present, you take away overthinking's fuel. Mainly, you are not dwelling on the past and you are not overly concerned about the future. Of course, it makes sense to prepare for the future. But then again, if you are prepared, then there's not much you need to worry about. You have everything you need to be ready. That way, when the future comes, you know what to do.

This is why the present is all about focus. This ties back to prioritization, your To-Do list, focus, concentration and being aware of your situation at present. When you are able to make all of these assessments, you realize that the present is the only thing that matters.

Why?

Because the present is the only thing you actually control. Moreover, when you declutter your lifestyle, it is so much easier to focus on the present simply because you have much less to worry about. If you have a number of balls in the air at the same time, it'll be hard for you to keep track of everything that's going on around you at any given time.

That leads to stress and anxiety... and it leads to overthinking things.

When you resolve to live in the present, you are not leaving the past behind nor are you neglecting the future; in fact, you are empowering yourself to use our most prize possession as efficiently as possible: time.

Time is the only commodity which we cannot get back once it is spent.

Chapter 32
Slow Down and Rewire your Brain to Be Yourself

Modern science has shown that the brain is a work in progress. What that means is that it is never fully developed. Of course, from childhood to adulthood, the brain matures enough to allow humans to carry out important biological functions.

This implies that the brain is hardly set in stone once you reach adulthood. In fact, whatever conditions you grew up in can be modified over time. While this takes a concerted effort to do so, it is by no means impossible. You have the power to consciously train your brain to do whatever you need it to do.

In the process of development and maturation, the brain develops its wiring, meaning, that it develops the neurological network that is responsible for activities such as language, critical thinking, motricity, and core biological functions.

For example, the brain is trained to function on eight hours of sleep a night. Yet, you can rewire your brain to function on less. Now, this doesn't mean that it will be functioning at optimum capacity, but it will get the job done. By the same token, you can rewire the brain once more to go back to functioning on more sleep.

So, if you find yourself consciously aware of the negative habits which you have acquitted over time, then the time has come for you to make a conscious effort to retrain your brain to do what you need it to do. This might mean develop new habits or curb older ones.

It does matter. What does matter is that you are able to make sense of the most important functions that you need to do when you need to do it. So, if you resolve to get up earlier and make the most of your day, then you can certainly train your brain to go to bed earlier and get up earlier. While that may not be the easiest thing in the world, it is certainly possible if you really set your mind to it.

This is possible of any habit and any skill you wish to develop in yourself.

Chapter 33
Create Good Habits

It very well may be difficult to manufacture great propensities.

These thoughts are not by any means the only method to manufacture great propensities — there are a lot of others out there — however, these straightforward advances can enable you to gain ground with a large portion of the objectives you have for your wellbeing, your work, and your life.

That is particularly valid if you need to stay with them as long as possible. Fortunately, there are a couple of basic systems that you can use to construct great propensities and break awful ones.

Also, in light of that, here are 3 things that you can do right presently to manufacture great propensities.

1. Build up an arrangement for when you fizzle.

Dan John, a prominent quality and molding mentor, regularly tells his competitors, "You're bad enough to be disillusioned." The equivalent is genuine when you construct another propensity. What were you anticipating? To prevail as a matter of course from the earliest starting point. To be impeccable in any event, when individuals who have been doing this for a considerable length of time commit errors all the time?

You need to figure out how to not pass judgment on yourself or feel regretful when you commit an error, and rather center around building up an arrangement to refocus as fast as could reasonably be expected.

Here are three systems that may help...

I discover the "never miss twice" mentality to be especially helpful. Perhaps I'll miss one exercise

Set calendars instead of cutoff time.

Disregard execution and spotlight on structure another character.

Make this your new saying: "Never miss twice."

I'm not going to miss two out of a column. Perhaps I'll eat a whole pizza, however, I'll line it up with a solid dinner. Perhaps I'll neglect to think today, yet tomorrow first thing I'll be overflowing with Zen.

Making mistakes on your propensities doesn't make you a disappointment. It makes you typical. What isolates top entertainers from every other person is that they refocus rapidly. Ensure you have an arrangement for when you fall flat.

   2. Start with a propensity that is so natural you can't state no.

The most significant piece of structure another propensity is remaining predictable. It doesn't make a difference how well you perform on any individual day. Continued exertion is the thing that has a genuine effect.

Therefore, when you start another propensity it ought to be anything but difficult to the point that you can't disapprove of it. Truth be told, when beginning another behavior is ought to be anything but difficult to such an extent that it's practically ludicrous.

Need to fabricate an activity propensity? You will probably practice for 1 moment today.

Need to begin a composition propensity? You will likely compose three sentences today.

Need to make a good dieting propensity? You will likely eat one solid supper this week.

It doesn't make a difference if you start little on the grounds that there will be a lot of time to get the power later. You don't have to join a CrossFit rec center, compose a book, or change your whole diet at the earliest reference point.

It's anything but difficult to contrast yourself with what others are doing or to want to improve your exhibition and accomplish more. Try not to give those sentiments a chance to pull you off-kilter. Demonstrate to yourself that you can adhere to something little for 30 days. At that point, when you are having some fantastic luck and staying predictable, you can stress over expanding the difficulty.

Initially, execution is superfluous. Accomplishing something amazing more than once won't make any difference if you never stay with it for them since a long time ago run. Make your new propensity so natural that you can't state no.

3. Set aside some effort to see precisely what is keeping you down.

I as of late talked with a lady named Jane. She needed to practice reliably, yet had consistently imagined that she was, in her words, "the kind of individual who didn't prefer to exercise."

Jane chose to bring an end to the propensity down and understood that it wasn't really practicing that troubled her. Rather, she didn't care for the issue of preparing for the rec center, driving someplace for 20 minutes, and after that working out. She likewise didn't appreciate setting off to an open spot and working out before other individuals. Those were the genuine hindrances that anticipated her activity propensity.

When she understood this, Jane contemplated how she could make practicing simpler. She purchased a yoga video and began practicing at home two evenings for each week. She was additionally an educator and her school offered an activity class for the staff after school. She began setting off to that class since it implied that she didn't need to drive elsewhere or put in a great deal of planning time just to exercise.

Jane has been adhering to her exercise routine throughout recent months. She says, "You probably won't have the option to fix all that you don't care for, however making sense of how to function around a couple of those obstacles may give the push you have to get past the halfway point and stick with your objectives."

The individuals who stick with great propensities see precisely what is keeping them down.

You may imagine that you're the "kind of individual who doesn't care for working out" or the "sort of individual who is sloppy" or the "sort of individual who surrenders to desires and eats desserts." But by and large, you're not bound to flop in those territories. Rather than owning a sweeping expression about your propensities, separate them into smaller pieces and consider which zones are keeping you from getting to be predictable.

When you know the specific pieces of the procedure that keep you down, you can start to build up an answer to tackle that issue.

Chapter 34
Do What you Love

How many times have you heard this one?

Sure, it might sound cliché, but it's actually true. There is something about doing what you love which makes life so much better.

Now, you might have heard this phrase related to work. After all, who wouldn't love to make a living doing what they love the most. Some people do, and some fail in the process.

Of course, doing what you love doesn't necessarily mean making a career out of it. It just means that you are making the most of your time partaking in activities that fulfill you; which gives you a sense of satisfaction and happiness.

For example, some folks find joy in the church. Attending their church service invigorates them and gives them a new lease on life. Others feel that way about sports, hobbies, travel and so on.

When you make a point of doing what you love, you are opening the door to a wonderful life in which you have control over what you wish to do with your time and your efforts. Naturally, we all need to make a living, pay bills and take care of our household. Still, these responsibilities don't preclude our ability to enjoy our lives.

So, make a point of taking the time to do the things that you love. Even if it is just one thing, at least you can make the time you need to enjoy life. Please bear in mind that life is fleeting. The next thing you know, it may be gone forever. The last thing that anyone wants is to live with regret, with a sense of longing for the time that was spent on other things.

After all, how many people have you heard regret not spending more time at the office while on their deathbed?

Chapter 35
Embrace Positive Influences with Positive Thinking

The universe is made up of energy. That energy is both positive and negative. What's more, both types of energy attract each other in such a way that positively charged energies attract other positively charged energy. The same can be said about negative energy.

In a practical sense, this means that when you charge your life with positive energy, the likelihood of you attracting more positive energy increases significantly. Conversely, if you charge up your negative energies, then that is what you shall attract.

Now, if your deal is to hang with negatively changed individuals, then by all means. But if you are looking to make a positive change in your life, then it is positive energy which you seek. This begins with making an effort to positively change your mindset.

To positively change your mindset, you can begin by flipping the narrative around. Let's assume that you have money problems and are in need of more cash. The obvious way to look at this issue would be, "I don't have any money. I need more money".

When you utter the words, "I don't have money", you are making a declaration to the universe that you lack. What this means is that you are embracing a scarcity mindset.

On the contrary, if you reframe the issue as "I have bills to pay. How can I make more money?" you are automatically making an affirmation to the universe that you are looking for opportunities.

Ask and you shall receive.

It's fairly straightforward.

So, make a point of cutting out "negatives" from your vocabulary. Make a point to make positive affirmations in spite of the situation. Stop saying, "I am sick" and embrace "I will be healed".

As Descartes said, "I think therefore I am".

Chapter 36
Remove Negative Influences
Cut Off Destroying Thoughts

Negative energy is everywhere. You can find it at every turn. Negative energy can take the form of unhappy people, violent content on television, or even environmental damage. You can see this on a consistent basis. No matter where you go, you will encounter charges of negative energy.

And while there isn't much you can do to stop negative energy from swirling around in the world, there is plenty which you can do to stop it from taking over your mind. In fact, when you find yourself immersed in a negative environment, it is very easy to get caught up in the negativity of the situation.

For instance, you are working in a very negative environment. Your boss and co-workers aren't getting along which leads to an overall unpleasant atmosphere. At this point, you have one of two choices, you either let that get to you, or you don't. Of course, it's not quite that simple.

One of the most effective ways to avoid being brought down by this type of atmosphere is to simply stop it from getting to you. You can learn to recognize the onset of negative thoughts and emotions. When you do, you can nip them in the bud. You can make use of mantras such as, "negative energies can't touch me" or "negative thoughts are like a ship passing in the night".

In other words, don't let negative thoughts pull up a chair and have a seat. If you allow them to do that, you are opening the door to trouble. The main thing to keep in mind is that you are the master of your thoughts and your emotions. The only way something can get to you is if you let it.

However, it is true that a highly negative environment will undoubtedly charge you with negative energy. In that case, it is always a great idea to have ways in which you can unload those energies. That is why pleasant activities are needed at the end of the day. That way, you can simply let go of the energies which are negatively affecting you.

Chapter 37
Getting Rid of Toxic People

Severally, we talk and spotlight on the significance of evacuating and getting rid of poisonous nourishment, films, and beverages, yet we overlook the significance of expelling dangerous individuals with lethal frames of mind from our lives. Much the same as every single other thing that is harmful in nature, poisonous individuals can harm and taint our lives with mental, enthusiastic and physical infections. Evacuating dangerous individuals can be difficult, particularly when we have a current association with them. Notwithstanding, here are a few hints that will enable you to evacuate any sort of lethal individual from your life:

1. Change your organization

One approach to treat the impact of awful things that have occurred in your life is to start to take in beneficial things. To dispose of poisonous individuals, encircle yourself with capable and beautiful individuals. The lethal individual will have no real option except to pull out.

There was a companion of mine who had a negative and lethal view concerning everything, so as to dispose of him, I warmed up to some folks with a ton of positive vibes. Sooner or later, I saw he barely came around me when I was with them. In the end, he left me.

Besides, through positive relations, you can enhance your shortcomings. You will likewise think that it is simpler to proceed onward from the hurt that negative and dangerous connections could have caused.

2. Be firm

Most harmful individuals resemble parasites, they don't do well without their host. This implies simply instructing them to leave your life probably won't be sufficient in light of the fact that they will consistently attempt to return. It is now that you should rehash your position without jumping. Your activities ought to likewise mirror your words (when you state "leave", you should avoid them yourself).

3. Gain as a matter of fact

After you have disposed of lethal connections, you need to gain from them. Hence, before beginning any genuine fellowship on a relationship, you should check such people for comparative characteristics. This will enable you to dispose of dangerous individuals for all time.

4. Structure plainly characterized limits

In managing poisonous individuals, it is significant that you defined limits concerning what they can do with you and what they can't. These limits must be upheld on the grounds that poisonous individuals consistently attempt to figure out how to sneak once again into your life. For instance, if you intend to restrict connections to simply welcome, guarantee that when they endeavor to raise a point for a discussion, you cut them off.

Obviously, this could be difficult, yet whatever merits doing at all merits progressing nicely. A few persuasive statements for understudies, laborers, educators, among others, express the significance of defining and keeping to limits, regardless of the expense.

5. Try not to be decent to them

At the point when we are attempting to expel an ailment from our body or attempting to get rid of dangerous nourishment or drink, we are not decent to it. The equivalent goes for poisonous individuals. Try not to grin to them, don't be delicate with them, rather, be exacting and solicit them to get out of your life.

This doesn't imply that you ought to turn into an awful or remorseless individual. Simply guarantee that your earnestness and stance leave no uncertainty of your aim in their brains.

6. Try not to attempt to transform them

Commonly, we fall into the snare of reasoning that it is our duty to change dangerous individuals or that they will in the end change. To dispose of them, you should be prepared to acknowledge that they won't change and that it isn't your obligation to endeavor to change their disposition. Interestingly, they generally appear to be happy to take exhortation and to change, yet they don't.

At the point when you quit searching for their salvation, it ends up simpler to desert them. I thought that it was difficult to leave a harmful relationship. This was on the grounds that consistently I woke up persuaded that the other individual was going to change. She didn't. I abandoned attempting to spare her so as to proceed onward.

7. Genuinely let them go (excuse)

Don't simply concentrate on physically disposing of a lethal individual, likewise, dispose of them inwardly. If a lethal individual hurt you, excuse the individual in your heart as you let the individual go. Along these lines, the individual doesn't stay to torment and harm you inwardly, even after they have left physically.

Keep in mind that generous them isn't overlooking that they are poisonous individuals, it is simply to enable your heart to proceed onward from them also. The absence of absolution is the reason numerous individuals are still overloaded from lethal connections that they are out of.

8. Identify the lethal nature

The absolute first activity in the voyage of disposing of dangerous individuals is to have the option to identify such individuals and how they are poisonous. Research has demonstrated a few attributes that will assist you in identifying a dangerous individual. You can view individuals as lethal when:

- They generally request that you substantiate yourself to them.

- They never apologize.

- They are manipulative.

- They are not steady.

- They never assume up liability.

- They are judgmental.

If you are in any type of relationship, where the individual shows any of such attributes (reliably), you are with a lethal individual. Realizing this is the initial step to being free.

9. Maintain a strategic distance from snares of emergencies

Harmful individuals consistently attempt to get again into your life or to remain thereby continually keeping you occupied with one emergency that happens in their life. To dispose of poisonous individuals, you should be prepared to turn away from their purported emergency and to proceed onward with your own life. Overlooking harmful individuals is a powerful method to get them to gather their packs and leave your life.

10. Know and claim your shortcomings and disappointments

Dangerous individuals are aces in the craft of misusing your disappointment for their own narrow-minded intrigue. Nonetheless, when you come to comprehend and acknowledge your shortcomings (with an offer to improve and turn out to be better), their hold over you falls flat. This makes the undertaking of showing them out of your life progressively effective.

Owning your shortcomings likewise incorporates putting stock in yourself and luxuriating in your quality and triumphs. This likewise causes you to see why your life is of an excessive amount of significant worth to permit dangerous individuals in it.

Lethal things are harmful things that can murder us if we don't dispose of them as fast and as proficiently as could be expected under the circumstances. Guarantee that you don't wait or proceed with that lethal companion or in that poisonous relationship anymore. It will enable you to live more. The tips recorded above will help you in escaping harmful connections.

Chapter 38
How to Stop Overthinking with Mindfulness Meditation

Folks who are unfamiliar with meditation believe it is some practice that monks do atop a mountain in the middle of nowhere. The fact of the matter is that you can practice meditation at any time, and in any place you choose.

One of the best to practice mindfulness meditation is when you are feeling overwhelmed by emotions, work, people, problems and so on. When you do this, you will be able to harness your emotions so that you can bring them back down to manageable levels. That way, when overthinking begins to creep in, you can stop it in its tracks.

Here is how mindfulness meditation works:

Let's say the action at work is getting hot and heavy. Naturally, you are consumed by the action and are beginning to have negative thoughts creep up behind you. So, what can you do?

Live in the here and the now.

Think about what the most important thing is at that moment. Think about why you feel why you do. And most importantly let go of the negativity that emerges from being in that situation.

Next, take a deep breath... you can literally count to 10. Each time you breathe in, close your eyes and visualize oxygen entering your lungs and charging your body with positive energy. Slowly exhale while you visualize a small black puff of smoke carry negativity away. This energy will dissolve in the air and disappear.

This practice does not need to take more than a couple of minutes. But that couple of minutes can be instrumental in helping you focus and keep negative thoughts at bay. Before you know it, you will have curbed negative feelings down to their least expression.

This can definitely help you stay focused while you get stuff done. Afterward, you can make the time for some self-care and unwind from the day you've had to deal with.

Chapter 39
What Is Mindfulness Meditation?

Have you at any point felt pushed, restless, or overpowered by life?

We live in a bustling world. With messages and messages flying all around as you are venturing over your kids' toys and attempting to get the canine sustained while the nourishment on the table is getting cold, you most likely get a handle on worried consistently.

Done effectively, mindfulness will enable you to diminish your pressure and nervousness, limit the measure of time that you spend feeling overpowered, and help you value every little minute as it occurs. In a universe of confusion, mindfulness may very well be the stunt you have to figure out how to have the option to adapt to the frenzy.

Luckily, there is a straightforward propensity you can use to normally quiet yourself down and acknowledge life more. It's called mindfulness. Mindfulness is the act of deliberately concentrating the majority of your consideration on the present minute and tolerating it without judgment. This is an incredible spot to begin if you are searching for the key component in joy.

If these sound like results you'd love to involvement, at that point I prescribe perusing this extreme manual for being careful about the duration of the day. First up, we'll spread the advantages of mindfulness—specifically, how it can decidedly affect both your mental and physical prosperity.

Advantages of Mindfulness

1. Mindfulness diminishes uneasiness

Research has discovered that mindfulness is particularly useful in diminishing nervousness. Rehearsing mindfulness consistently revamps your cerebrum so you can refocus your consideration. As opposed to following a negative and stressing thought down a way of every single imaginable result, you can figure out how to see the truth about your contemplations and simply let them go.

2. Mindfulness improves memory, focus, and execution

Focusing and focusing on the job that needs to be done might be one of the most significant psychological capacities individuals have. Mindfulness is one of the not very many strategies that function as a remedy for mind-meandering and the negative impacts that losing focus may have on you. Truth be told, inquire about understudies has demonstrated that there is an association among mindfulness and focusing both all through the study hall.

Extra examinations have demonstrated that ruminating over a standard premise causes the cerebrum's cerebral cortex (which is answerable for memory, fixation, and figuring out how) to thicken.

3. Mindfulness gives relief from discomfort

Around 100 million Americans experience the ill effects of ceaseless torment each day, yet 40% to 70% of these individuals are not accepting legitimate medicinal treatment. Numerous investigations have demonstrated that mindfulness contemplation can decrease torment without utilizing endogenous narcotic frameworks that are generally accepted to diminish torment during subjective based systems like mindfulness.

Oneself created narcotic framework has as a rule been suspected of as the focal piece of the mind for mitigating torment without the utilization of medications. This framework self-produces three narcotics, including beta-endorphin, the met-and Leu-enkephalins, and the dynorphins. These work together to lessen torment by rehearsing mindfulness.

4.   Mindfulness assists with passionate reactivity

Of the considerable number of reasons that individuals more often than not have for learning contemplation, being less sincerely receptive is normally high on the rundown. Being careful or "Zen" compares to moving with the punches in life and being non-receptive to things that may come to your direction.

What's more, there's unquestionably something to this. Mindfulness contemplation has permitted study members to remove their feelings from upsetting pictures and spotlight more on an intellectual errand, as contrasted and a control gathering.

5.   Mindfulness decreases rumination and overthinking

One of the most well-known manifestations that join tension is rumination or overthinking. After you start to stress over something, your mind will clutch that firmly and make it difficult to give up. It is anything but difficult to get into an idea circle where you keep on replaying every single awful result possible. We as a whole realize this isn't valuable since stressing over something doesn't keep it from occurring.

One investigation really demonstrated that individuals who were new to mindfulness and started to rehearse it during a retreat had the option to give fewer indications of rumination and uneasiness than the control gathering.

6. Mindfulness makes more joyful connections

Scientists are as yet uncertain this works, yet rising cerebrum studies have demonstrated that individuals who take part in mindfulness all the time show both auxiliary and useful changes in the mind locales that are connected to improved sympathy, empathy, and generosity.

Another advantage of mindfulness is in its impacts on the amygdala, which is the cerebrum's enthusiastic preparing focus. Mindfulness is connected to decreases in both the volume of the amygdala and its association with the prefrontal cortex. This recommends mindfulness may bolster feeling guidelines and lessening reactivity, which are two significant devices for making and looking after connections.

6. Mindfulness improves rest

The unwinding reaction that your body needs to mindfulness reflection is a remarkable inverse of the pressure reaction. This unwinding reaction attempts to ease many pressures related to medical problems, for example, agony, wretchedness, and hypertension. Rest issues are regularly attached to these illnesses.

One investigation of more established grown-ups affirms that mindfulness contemplation can help in getting a decent night's rest. As indicated by this examination, mindfulness reflection can expand the unwinding reaction through its capacity of expanding attentional components that confer command over the autonomic sensory system.

9. Mindfulness eases some pressure

Since individuals are looked with an expanding measure of weight nowadays because of the mind-boggling nature of our general public, they are regularly tormented with a ton of stress. This adds to a wide assortment of other medical issues. Mindfulness can diminish worry by going about as a precaution measure, and help individuals overcome difficult occasions.

10. Mindfulness advances mental wellbeing

Specialists have discovered that IBMT (integrative body-mind preparing) starts positive auxiliary changes in the cerebrum that could help secure against mental infection. The act of this strategy helps support productivity in a piece of the cerebrum that enables individuals to direct behavior.

11. Mindfulness advances intellectual adaptability

One examination proposes that not exclusively will mindfulness help individuals become less receptive; it may likewise give individuals progressively intellectual adaptability. Individuals who practice mindfulness seem, by all accounts, to be ready to likewise rehearse self-perception, which consequently withdraws the pathways made in the cerebrum from earlier learning and permits data that is going on right now to be comprehended in another manner.

Reflection additionally enacts the piece of the mind that is related to versatile reactions to push, which compares to a quicker recuperation to a benchmark line of reasoning in the wake of being contrarily affected.

Chapter 40
How to Meditate Your Worries Away

We are instructed to move away from dread—to pick comfort and quick fulfillment over the hard way. But then, we who ruminate are continually picking the hard way. Confidence is a position of a riddle, where we discover the boldness to have faith in what we can't see and the solidarity to relinquish our dread of vulnerability.

Each time I go into contemplation, it is a demonstration of trust, of squeezing into dread and drawing nearer to reality. It is the act of contemplating that has enabled me to look for that reality, to pick the harder way, and to discover sympathy for myself all the while.

As the years progressed, I've gone over a couple of sorts of contemplation that have helped me in the most dread ridden times of my life.

Qigong Meditation

In Traditional Chinese Medicine, it is accepted that dread is put away in the kidneys. In Western medication, it is realized that frightful considerations are minimal more than compound and electrical sign, activated through a mind-boggling system of correspondence in the body's cells. With enough reiteration, those neural pathways are framed and established, causing a similar reaction each time a danger is recognized.

Sit with your shoulders and your feet level against the floor. Spot your hands over your kidneys (at your back under your lower ribs). Picture them and the little adrenal organs over them in your psyche.

At the point when the psyche is looked with a danger, regardless of whether genuine or saw, it revisits those pathways to do similar activities. Furthermore, that is the place qigong contemplation steps in. By rehashing positive musings, you can make and fortify neural pathways, and clear up the kidneys, to assist you with more noteworthy authority over your feelings.

After a couple of breath cycles, lean forward a little as you breathe in, catch your hands beneath your knees, open your eyes, and envision breathing out dread, making a "choo" sound.

Closer your eyes, grin, and breathe in your stomach out envisioning dull blue light and harmony encompassing your kidneys and adrenal organs. Breathe out by driving your stomach back in.

Lean In

The act of reflection is intended to be down to earth in helping us travel during our time with a touchstone of harmony and mindfulness. Similarly, as with any feeling, contemplation can help balance out us notwithstanding trepidation to enable us to comprehend it all the more unmistakably.

As the day progressed, you can enable yourself to meet dread in an increasingly positive manner with the intensity of reflection.

Check-in with your feelings consistently. At whatever point you feel dreadful, let the inclination remain.

Rather than running, adopt a full breath and strategy your contemplations of fear and stress with neighborliness and interest. Be thoughtful to yourself in dread, as you would for a confided in companion.

If you have the opportunity and space, plunk down and inhale into your dread for ten breath cycles.

Dread AS POWER

Dread is stating that this is the ideal time to have the option to do what you're attempting to do. Your body is really setting you up to have a positive result. When you can truly comprehend that dread is a feeling like some other feeling, you can figure out how to oversee it. And afterward, you can accomplish things that the vast majority consider to be exceptional.

To beat my dread of statures, I have grasped the fear, taking a lead shake climbing class where I need to move to the highest point of the divider and free fall mostly down the divider before being securely gotten with a rope.

Through training, receptiveness, and cheering companions and teachers, I have figured out how to inhale through the dread and let go again and again. The dread remains, however my response to it has changed.

Practice it yourself — what is your dread? What little, safe advances would you be able to take to work on disapproving of your breath in that dread? As you practice, what changes do you see after some time?

Chapter 41
Mindfulness in Everyday Life

As we have pointed out earlier, mindfulness is not some practice limited to monks who have taken a vow of silence. This is the type of practice which virtually anyone can do, at any time, and anywhere.

So, here are some additional strategies to implement mindfulness in your everyday life:

1. Sit with your experience

At the point when you center around being careful, you can sit with your experience.

Rehearsing mindfulness through concentrating on your body, psyche, and soul will enable you to turn out to be all the more dominant. The more you do this, the more you shut out the sense of self and the better you will feel in all pieces of yourself.

With shut eyes and a casual body, center around your relaxing. Tune in for sounds that are close by or even far away. Output your body to get a feeling of what is loose and what is holding strain. If you have a tingle, see the tingle however don't attempt to transform it. Simply travel through it.

This is a great practice for simply being careful without attempting to take care of business.

Once in a while, life is awkward like a tingle. Sitting with the experience will enable you to see that things go back and forth.

Nervousness can sneak up in your paunch or you may encounter a snugness in your throat while you reflect.

The brain is telling the body that there are such a large number of activities. At the point when you do encounter strain in the body, you can contact that zone with your hands and inside the state, "This as well." You're recognizing your full understanding without attempting to transform it. This is mindfulness.

Let's assume you're sitting outside in a recreation center; all is well until you see two individuals unmistakably enamored. Abruptly, dejection kicks in and no one is around to facilitate the inclination. This bit of dejection has consistently been in your heart.

It's not constantly enacted however can emerge at any minute. You become feeble and it feels like your heart is sinking. Different occasions you've felt alone are activated and put away vitality from the past strikes a chord.

How would you take care of the issue without calling somebody or utilizing an old device to calm down your contemplations and sentiments?

Basically, see that you took notes. You are the subject and you are what takes note. Those sentiments of the void are objects. Out is to see who is feeling the torment and depression. Give the emotions a chance to go through without fleeing or staying away from them.

Mindfulness doesn't mean getting to be associated with the show of the psyche. It's tied in with seeing the manner in which the psyche and body are reacting with full acknowledgment.

The touchy individual in you who has had numerous encounters will feel apprehensive, destitute, and desirous every once in a while. This is the mind and the conscience affecting everything. You are the person who is careful, you are the inhabiting being who knows.

To take advantage of the piece of you that sits looking out for this human experience, you simply need to remain completely focused.

All of what I'm stating may appear to be exceptionally perplexing for some who have never polished mindfulness. It just requires some investment of not responding and rather watching your experience to comprehend the procedure I'm discussing.

Reflection is an incredible practice for minutes that bring awkward feelings.

2. Attempt this activity

Make proper acquaintance with the one in your brain. Just inside make proper acquaintance. Who makes proper acquaintance and who hears hi? It's you who's talking and it's you who's tuning in.

The most ideal approach to turn out to be free from the steady prattle that is bolstering your horrendous thoughts is to step back. Take a gander at it dispassionately. Musings are only an object of the psyche, something that should drift by and not be clutched or dismissed.

As you're careful and watch the voice, you'll start to see that the greater part of what it says has next to no significance. It complains about the past and utilizes old encounters to attempt to control present and future encounters. This causes a wide range of issues in your life.

If you need to turn out to be free from your own brain, you must be careful enough to truly observe what's happening up there. At the point when you discover that a lot of your activities originating from some nonsensical voice that wants comfort, you can start to settle on different choices.

All in all, mindfulness can mend numerous things yet how would we accomplish it? One of the pathways to calm the psyche and go within ourselves is through contemplation.

3. Everyday contemplation

Contemplation isn't difficult but then its effortlessness threatens many.

This is on the grounds that your self-image wouldn't like to be calmed. It reveals to you that you're excessively occupied, that reflection is inconsequential, and that it's excessively unusual and otherworldly for you.

What's truly going on is that the self-image is terrified of ending up calm. Backing off and going in methods there's the capability of standing up to awkward sentiments. You gave your sense of self the activity of keeping away from distress or saw peril.

At the point when we ponder, there is incredible danger of running into past torment.

Mindfulness through your contemplation enables you to at long last manage old injuries so you don't need to live with them any longer. That implies that they never again have power over you.

To develop mindfulness, you'll need to invest significant energy consistently, yet this shouldn't be a task. The mind will prattle and reveal to you it's exhausted. Simply continue watching the objects of musings and emotions traveling through you.

The more you practice, the more you'll anticipate having that uninterrupted alone time. Consider it daily in the spa or getting a back rub. When you get into it, that focused inclination makes you feel as loose as 40 minutes in a sauna.

While you'll start to experience benefits practically immediately, the more you practice mindfulness, the more noteworthy the advantages will be.

In both the Buddhist ways of thinking and present-day psychotherapy, mindfulness is accomplished through reflection.

There is a wide range of approaches to reflect as well, so don't sit in lotus posture and consume those incense sticks at this time. Reflection is the umbrella for mending and inside your contemplations, you can accomplish numerous things for the body, psyche, and soul.

Mindfulness contemplation isn't tied in with changing or modifying yourself in any capacity. It's tied in with getting to be mindful of what your identity is. As you sit peacefully, things will come up. As you search inside yourself, recollections may come up as if they are a motion picture on a screen.

If you remain in the seat of cognizance without getting sucked in, you can become familiar with a great deal. You'll know if you get sucked in on the grounds that you won't let pictures go. You'll get genuinely included and pressure will begin to develop.

Buddha said that the wellspring of your enduring is attempting to flee from your immediate experience. Remaining in a lovely minute from your past is equivalent to pieces of torment. Clutching things keeps you before and it's essentially not beneficial for your mind.

Chapter 42
A Simple Mindfulness Meditation
Practice to Relieve Stress and Anxiety

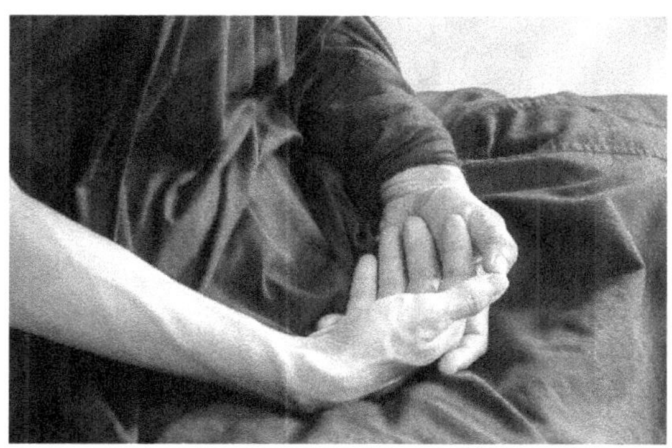

The most fundamental approach to do careful breathing is essential to concentrate on your breath, then breathe in and breathe out. You can do this while standing, yet preferably you'll be sitting or in any event, lying in an agreeable position. Your eyes might be open or shut, however, you may think that it is simpler to keep up your concentration if you close your eyes. It can save an assigned time for this activity; however, it can likewise rehearse it when you're feeling especially pushed or restless. Specialists accept a customary routine with regards to careful breathing can make it simpler to do it in difficult circumstances.

Once in a while, particularly when attempting to quiet yourself in a distressing minute, it may begin by taking an overstated breath: a profound breath in through your noses

(3 seconds), hold your breath (2 seconds), and a long breath out through your mouth (4 seconds). Something else, essentially watch every breath without attempting to alter it; it might concentrate on the ascent and fall of your chest or the sensation through your noses. As you do as such, you may find that your mind meanders, diverted by contemplations or substantial sensations. That is OK. Simply see this is occurring and delicately take your consideration back to your breath.

To give considerably more structure, and help you lead this training for other people, underneath are ventured for a short-guided reflection. You can tune in to the sound of this guided reflection, created by UCLA's Mindful Awareness Research Center (MARC), in the player underneath; if it doesn't play, you can discover it here or download it from MARC's site.

Tune into your breath. Feel the regular progression of breath—in, out. You don't have to do anything to your breath. Not long, not short, simply characteristic. Notice where you feel your breath in your body. It may be in your belly. It might be in your chest or throat or in your noses. Check whether you can feel the vibes of breath, each breath in turn. At the point when one breath closes, the following breath starts.

Locate a casual, agreeable position. You could be situated on a seat or on the floor on a pad. Keep your back upstanding, yet not very tight. Hands resting any place they're agreeable. Tongue on the top of your mouth or any place it's agreeable.

Notice and loosen up your body. Attempt to see the state of your body, its weight. Allow yourself to unwind and wind up inquisitive about your body situated here—the sensations it encounters, the touch, the association with the floor or the seat. Loosen up any zones of snugness or strain. Simply relax.

Presently as you do this, you may see that your psyche may begin to meander. You may begin contemplating different things. If this occurs, it's anything but an issue. It's exceptionally characteristic. Simply see that your brain has meandered. You can say "thinking" or "meandering" in your mind delicately. And after that tenderly divert your consideration right back to the relaxing.

Remain here for five to seven minutes. Notice your breath, peacefully. Every once in a while, you'll lose all sense of direction in idea, at that point come back to your breath.

Following a couple of minutes, indeed see your body, your entire body, situated here. Give yourself a chance to unwind much more profoundly and after that offer yourself some gratefulness for doing this training today.

Chapter 43
Mindfulness Exercises for A Good Sleep

Mindfulness reflection offers a novel and compelling way to deal with feeling guidelines and stress decrease that can drastically improve rest designs.

Normal, customary nervousness and stress can prompt rest issues in youngsters. Youngsters may experience difficulty nodding off or staying unconscious and may wind up on edge about their issue resting. Research demonstrates that mindfulness-based activities significantly increment rest time, lessen a sleeping disorder and lower pre-rest excitement levels. One investigation found that understudies who took an interest in Tai-Chi expanded their mindfulness as well as improved their rest quality. Another investigation of ninth-grade girls encountering poor rest found that mindfulness preparing improved rest beginning, rest productivity, and complete rest time. The understudies hit the sack before and woke before also.

Mindfulness contemplation was initially created as a preparation technique for expanding mindfulness. By expanding mindfulness right now, people can shift their regard for what is, as opposed to stress over what may be. Mindfulness and acknowledgment help introduce the "giving up" that enables rest to normally happen.

Here are a few hints for managing your kids through mindfulness contemplation exercises to help slip them into the joyful place that is known for Nod.

For offspring everything being equal, put aside a couple of minutes before sleep time, in a perfect world simultaneously every night, to take part in a genuine talk. Give the youngster a chance to trust their issues and fears. Offer consolation and compassion, and an embrace or cuddle if fitting. At that point start a mindfulness work out. Guardians and kids can take part in these activities together the initial couple of times, and afterward, later the youngster might be happy with starting activities all alone.

Turning Off Meditation

This can pursue a resting contemplation. Notice the sentiment of the body on the bed. Feel the warm body sinking into the bedding. Notice where the body feels overwhelming and where it feels light. Notice the little toe of the left foot and envision it will rest for the evening. Give it consent to turn off for the evening. Do likewise for each toe on the left foot, at that point the impact point, wad of the foot, lower leg, calf, knee, and thigh. Presently, breathe out and see how the whole left leg is loose, substantial, and warm. Rehash this turning off exercise with the correct leg. Proceed up through the pelvis, gut, chest, and down the arms, into the hands and fingers. Drift off to rest.

Situated Mindful Breathing

Sit on an agreeable seat, reflection pad, or the edge of the bed. Drop the jaw somewhat, let the eyes close. Pursue the breath as it streams gradually in and out. Feel air traveling through the nose and mouth. Notice the stomach and chest rising and afterward falling. Focus on the quiet interruption before every inward breath. If the mind meanders, simply return consideration tenderly to the breath. Profound, delicate, slow breathing can loosen up the body and moderate the heart.

Adoring Kindness Meditation

After careful breathing, an offspring of all ages can get cherishing generosity by thinking about an individual near them who adores them profoundly. Regardless of whether a parent, relative, companion or even somebody who has passed on, they can picture that individual alongside them, grinning and sending adoration and warmth. They ought to wait over the affection that is exuding from that individual's general existence. Feeling that affection, they should now infer a second individual who appreciates them and envisions that individual remaining by them on the opposite side, simply radiating out adoration and security. At long last, they can infer everybody who cherishes and thinks about them—their preferred instructor, their closest companion, their pet—and envision them all assembled, sending wants for joy and wellbeing. They can feel in their heart and chest region all the glow, wellbeing, joy and delight of being cherished.

In the second piece of a cherishing thoughtfulness reflection, a youngster can send that adoration back to every individual, beginning with the first they envisioned. They can feel their very own heart growing, loaded up with happiness and love that streams out to other people.

Resting Mindful Breathing

Untruth serenely in bed and take in profoundly and completely. Feel the lungs load up with air. Notice the chest and midsection rising. Presently breathe out and let the emotions and stresses of the day stream out with the breath and vanish like wisps on the breeze. If stresses emerge once more, acknowledge them without judgment and breathe out them delicately with the breath, seeing them skim away and disappear. Presently envision breathing out to the edge of the sky or skyline and after that breathing from that point once again into the body. This activity can shift the body to a quiet and-interface state.

Chapter 44
Active Problem Solving
Think Smarter

When faced with an issue, a large number of us like to stall or stay away from the issue out and out. Dodging issues is a momentary arrangement. Critical thinking keeps you pushing ahead. It's basic for completing work. Along these lines, the quicker you can tackle any issue, the quicker you can complete the work or audit the answer to guarantee it's right (and return home on schedule).

So, here are some useful tips that can get your creative juices flowing.

1. Investigation

Obviously, look into alone isn't sufficient. Consider inquiring about the field where you've planted the seed of information, yet it's the worked over that nursery, the watering and sustaining that uncovers natural product. That worked is an investigation. It's a method to take what you know and use it to comprehend why something isn't continuing as it should. The examination comes in numerous structures, regardless of whether it's money-saving advantage investigation, hole examination or whatever other structure that encourages you to comprehend your present state.

Systematic aptitudes enable you to see a circumstance and draw based on what is frequently turbulent wreckage, the center issue that is causing the issue. This critical thinking ability gives you a pathway through the issue, so you can create powerful answers for determination.

These scientific aptitudes are not simply useful for triage; however, it helps, yet they can likewise help to precede the issue when you're in the exploration arrange. The issue with research is realizing what is significant and what is not. Expository aptitudes give you the devices to organize viably, as time is consistent with the quintessence with any serious issue.

2. Exercise

There are practices you can do to pick up critical thinking aptitudes and help with your capacity to all the more likely react to issues and fathom them rapidly. For instance, there are rationale thinking tests that help sort out your contemplations obviously, dissect them and pick the best game-plan rapidly. These tests will enable you to perceive and maintain a strategic distance from the run of the mill intelligent misrepresentations.

Spatial-transient thinking tests your capacity to mentally picture objects, which is critical to effectively see space and situating ourselves. Numerical thinking encourages us to get, structure, arrange and take care of issues with scientific techniques or equations. Consistent thinking likewise assists with critical thinking aptitudes in that it offers different recommendations by utilizing what we definitely know and what we accept to know and even what we don't have the foggiest idea.

There a lot more instances of when rationale works out, yet before you even start testing yourself and improving your critical thinking abilities, it's imperative to deal with yourself. Make certain to adhere to a decent rest plan, do ordinary physical activities, keep a thought diary to encourage imaginative reasoning, even have a go at doing yoga or a reflective practice. Everything primes your body and mind and improve your critical thinking abilities.

3. Imagination

Imagination—it's not only for specialists. Inventiveness is basically having the option to discover an answer that is novel. This implies not reacting to issues with an automatic response, or some sheltered arrangement that will probably bring unacceptable outcomes.

What imagination calls for is having the option to take a gander at an issue from numerous points of view, not simply the one you're OK with. You've heard the adages: step out of your customary range of familiarity, consider new ideas, redefine known limits. All things considered, there's some reality to these announcements, regardless of whether they've been rehashed to the point of silliness.

Things being what they are, what are imaginative reasoning aptitudes? Conceptualizing for one. It opens the talk to more than your perspective and broadens the focal point to open a more extensive perspective on the scene. Conceptualizing is a kind of joint effort, which is an incredible method to think inventively in light of the fact that it adds more voices to the blend. In any case, don't hang tight for motivation. Keep in mind, you have to get into the everyday practice, so when motivation hits you can misuse it. Have a go at utilizing innovativeness activities to get into the mind-set.

4. Perfect

Before we leave the subject, we should share one critical thinking system you can attempt then next opportunity an issue comes up that you should manage. The IDEAL strategy is an abbreviation that represents Identify (the issue), Define (the snags), Examine (your alternatives), Act (on a concurred game-plan) and Look (how it turns out and whether any progressions are required).

This procedure fuses quite a bit of what has just been examined and gives an unmistakable layout to tending to issues and rapidly settling them. At the point when you identify the issue, get notification from everybody in the group. At that point characterize the obstructions as well as your objectives in settling it. The investigation of potential arrangements should take a gander at if it will work, yet if it's sheltered, sensible, the best arrangement, and so forth. When an answer has been concurred on follow up on it.

What we've not talked about, which is a piece of the IDEAL strategy, is the last advance, Learn. Whatever strategy is taken, it's basic to screen and cover how it functioned or didn't function. If it doesn't work, at that point return to the start and start new. This will likewise educate you on what to do and what not to do whenever a comparable issue occurs.

5. Choosing

It sounds silly, yet one of the boundaries to taking care of an issue is having the option to act and settle on a choice. Research and investigation are significant, obviously, however, if you fall prey to examination loss of motion, at that point the issues endure. Thinking about an issue and talking about how to react to it is ineptitude without settling on something.

Some may state anything is superior to sitting idle, and there's some reality to that, yet the choice must be based on the exploration with the systematic slashes so as to have the impact you need. You should assess what is the best arrangement, and there will be multiple, so you'll need to pick what is most reasonable and sensible.

Would you be able to settle on that choice rapidly? With experience, you'll be progressively ready to act quick. If you don't have a lot of understanding, at that point the examination and systematic abilities are an extraordinary weight to keep you above water and cruising the correct way in the midst of the tempests that issues work up. Overhauling your basic leadership procedure is probably the quickest approach to improve your critical thinking, so know about how and for what reason you're settling on your choices.

6. Research

Research means doing the due steadiness before setting out on executing your venture, and it is the stone on which all your critical thinking sits. Consequently, to not put it down as a fundamental aptitude that all great issue solvers share for all intents and purpose would leave a major opening in your critical thinking abilities.

Issues, as a rule, don't appear without a history, and where there's a history, there's likewise a point of reference for reacting to the issue. To comprehend the manner in which others fixed an issue is to discover an exit from the one you're in now.

Be that as it may, there's additional. The more profound your examination, the more uncertain you'll have an issue in any case. That and the way that your commonality with a procedure will improve you ready to identify an issue before it turns into an issue. Conceptualizing with your group just extends the information base and improves critical thinking, particularly if they're encountered and have leaked that experience into the research of their own.

7. Correspondence

As with nearly everything, there is no hope without the informative aptitudes to convey the answer for the individuals who must purpose it. Interchanges appear to be simple until you attempt to convey. Indeed, even straightforward thoughts are frequently obfuscated by poor talk, also the mess that accompanies attempting to hand-off complex ones and take care of issues.

It's not simply having the option to convey plainly to orders yet realizing the correct channel to impart your message is likewise significant. That message needs to go to the correct individuals and contact them at the earliest opportunity. Finding an answer for an issue is just one connection in a bigger chain. If that arrangement isn't conveyed to the gatherings that need it to fix the issue for the undertaking to push ahead, at that point all is in vain. Attempt our free correspondence plan format to plainly guide out your interchanges.

Not every person is brought into the world an incredible communicator, however, there are approaches to figure out how to impart better. It takes sympathy and undivided attention to create trust and unwaveringness. Without that security between a group, regardless of how expressly you convey your message, it will be misheard or even overlooked.

Chapter 45

Critical Thinking to Improve Problem-Solving and Decision-Making Tips

1. See potential reasons for the issue

It's astounding the amount you don't think about what you don't have a clue. Consequently, in this stage, it's basic to get a contribution from other individuals who notice the issue and who are affected by it.

It's regularly valuable to gather contributions from different people each in turn (in any event from the outset). Something else, individuals will, in general, be hindered about offering their impressions of the genuine reasons for issues.

Record what your sentiments and what you've gotten notification from others.

Concerning you think maybe execution issues related to a worker, it's regularly valuable to look for exhortation from a friend or your boss so as to verify your impression of the issue.

Record a depiction of the reason for the issue and as far as what's going on, where, when, how, with whom and why.

2. Plan the usage of the best option (this is your activity plan)

Cautiously consider "What will the circumstance resemble when the issue is comprehended?"

What steps ought to be taken to execute the best option in contrast to tackling the issue? What frameworks or procedures ought to be changed in your association, for instance, another strategy or technique? Try not to depend on arrangements where somebody is "simply going to invest more energy".

In what manner will you know if the means are being pursued or not? (these are your pointers of the achievement of your arrangement)

What assets will you need as far as individuals, cash, and offices?

What amount of time will you have to execute the arrangement? Compose a calendar that incorporates the beginning and stop times, and when you hope to see certain markers of accomplishment.

Who will fundamentally be answerable for guaranteeing the execution of the arrangement?

Record the responses to the above inquiries and consider this as your activity plan.

Convey the arrangement to the individuals who will be engaged with executing it and, at any rate, to your prompt director.

3. Select a way to deal with determination the issue

When choosing the best approach, consider:

Which approach is the well on the way to take care of the issue as long as possible?

Which approach is the most sensible to achieve for the present? Do you have the assets? Is it true that they are reasonable? Do you have sufficient opportunity to execute the methodology?

What is the degree of hazard related to every option?

4. Identify options for ways to deal with purpose the issue

Now, it's valuable to keep others included (except if you're confronting an individual and additionally worker execution issue). Conceptualize for answers for the issue. Simply put, conceptualizing is gathering whatever number thoughts as could be expected under the circumstances, at that point screening them to locate the best thought. It's basically when gathering the plans to not pass any judgment on the thoughts - simply record them as you hear them. (A superb arrangement of abilities used to identify the basic reason for issues is Systems Thinking.)

Chapter 46

Focus on the Problem You Are Solving

Effective problem-solving skills generally call for you to focus on the actual situation you are trying to deal with. Often, you might get insights regarding other issues that might be related to the task at hand. However, if you allow your attention to dissipate toward other issues, you will be doing yourself a disservice by letting your creative energies distribute unevenly.

When you are able to focus on one issue at a time, you will find that you can solver things a lot more effectively than if your mind was meandering about. Hence, your attention is the most prized commodity in this regard.

Here is one short and effective strategy which can help you: time blocking.

While there are times when you need to think on your feet and make decisions in real-time, often, most issues will allow you enough time to sit down and go over it. Of course, when you are faced with life-or-death problems, you may no choice but to go with your instincts. But the fact of the matter is that most situations can be put off until a better time.

This is where you can block off your time. You can set aside a fixed amount of time to deal with that problem. This may be 30 minutes one morning, it might mean getting up earlier one day to work on it, or it might even mean clearing an entire afternoon. Whatever the time you need, you can try your best to clear it up. That way, you will be able to focus solely on this.

Also, don't be afraid to brainstorm ideas while you are at it. Often, some of the most outrageous ideas end up becoming viable alternatives to problems that you have been struggling to solve. So, take the time to go over your ideas and contemplate the best course of action. Please keep in mind that the more time you are able to devote to an issue, the easier it will become to solve.

Chapter 47
Find Simple Solutions

Have you ever heard of "Occam's Razor"?

Occam's Razor is a philosophical axiom that states: the simplest solution is usually the right one.

While you might be thinking that it is an over-simplistic view of reality, the fact is that the best solution is often simple and low-tech. Sure, solving some of the world's biggest problems has required humankind's cleverest minds. But often, some of the world's biggest issues have been solved with a very mundane solution.

If we translate this to everyday life, your problems, no matter how complex they are, can be boiled down to a simple and effective solution.

For instance, you are struggling financially. So, you are clear about the fact that you need more money. A highly complicated solution would be to become a cyberterrorist and digitally rob a bank.

That seems kind of convoluted, doesn't it?

However, you consider other low-tech solutions. Based on this, you choose to sell t-shirts. While that is hardly the sexiest business out there, it is the kind of business that has been proven to generate revenue. Alternatively, you choose to suck it up and get another job.

Of course, these solutions might not make you rich, but they will be enough to get you out from behind the eight-ball.

The beauty of implementing a low-tech, low-risk, low-complication approach is that it allows you to build layers on the complexity on top of them. So, you can start out by selling t-shirts at a local flea market. As you progress, you can migrate to an online empire. The ultimate point is that you are able to make things more suited to your particular condition as you gain experience.

So, don't be afraid to start off small. After all, how many of the world's largest corporations started out in a garage?

Chapter 48
Make Fact-based decisions

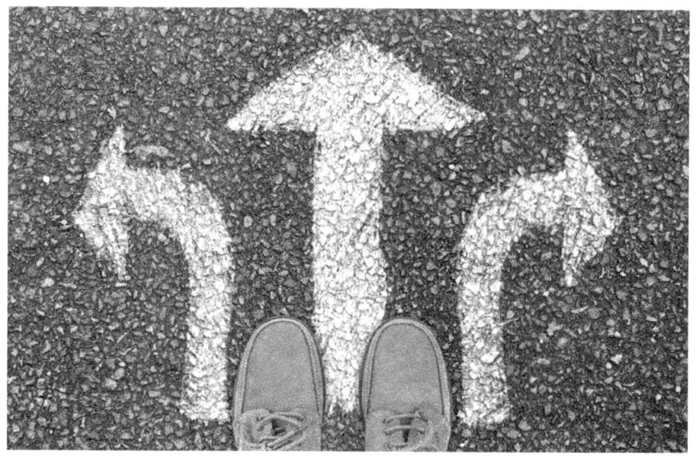

For all the gut an intuition out there, the truth is that making decisions based on fact are always guaranteed to be more effective than those based on assumptions. In fact, some of the world's biggest mistakes have been made when basing decisions on assumptions.

In the financial world, speculation can make investors insanely rich overnight. If they guess right, they can make their retirement with a few keystrokes. However, if they are wrong, they can end up in jail.

That is why savvy investors base their decisions on numbers, financials, and solid technical analysis. If the numbers don't paint the right picture, the savvy investor is prepared to leave a deal on the table.

Now, learning to listen to your gut is important. Yet, listening to your gut is a skill that becomes sharpened with experience. As you learn throughout the course of your life, your instincts tell you when something is on the up and up, or if there is something fishy. It isn't some magical sixth sense; it's your experience telling you what might be a good opportunity from a poor choice.

At the end of the day, your decisions ought to be based on the information you have on hand at any given moment. For instance, if you are planning to make a large purchase and you are betting on a future raise or promotion which may, or may not happen, then you are asking for trouble.

If you base your decision on the information you have available at the time of making a said decision, you will err on the side of caution. So, if you do end up getting that promotion, you won't have to sweat it. You will have extra money to play around with. However, if you bet on getting that promotion, and it doesn't happen, you'll find yourself in a pickle when it comes time to pay up.

So, always base your decisions on fact, not assumptions, and you'll come up a winner each time.

Chapter 49
Stop Overthinking for an Easier and Happier Life

At this point, there is one more thing to be said: overcoming any tendencies to overthink will lead you to a happier and easier life.

How is this possible?

Think about it along these lines: the amount of brainpower that you are freeing up will allow you to focus on the truly productive and truly valuable things in life. You will be able to get ahead in your profession and cherish the moments with your loved ones.

Naturally, everything must come to an end at some point. But if you stop dwelling on the fact that your loved one might leave you one day, and instead opt for treasuring the time they are actually with you, you will find that living a happy and productive life is not nearly as hard as you might have once thought.

You have everything you need to be happy and successful. It's just that we often make the mistake of misallocating your time and energy on fruitless endeavors. When you learn to see such activities for what they are, you will become a much more balanced and centered person.

While overthinking will creep up to you from time to time, the truth is that you shouldn't let it become more important than it ought to be.

So, please look at life's problems in terms of opportunities rather than problems. When you look at life in terms of opportunities, the world magically opens up. Since you are not dwelling on the issue itself, but rather on the solution, you can pick and choose from the worst, and certainly the best, options available to you.

Then, when you are able to solve the problem at hand, you will come out of it a much more experienced and interesting person. You will be able to offer the world the fruits of your efforts.

What could be better than that?

Conclusion

Thank you for making it through to the end of *Overthinking*, let's hope it was informative and able to provide you with all of the tools you need to achieve your goals whatever they may be.

The next step is to put to practice what you have learned.

Finally, if you found this book useful in any way, a review on Amazon is always appreciated!

www.ingramcontent.com/pod-product-compliance
Lightning Source LLC
Chambersburg PA
CBHW070658250726
48662CB00001B/184